THE PASSING OF
THE GREAT WEST

The Passing of the
GREAT WEST

→────────────────────←

SELECTED PAPERS OF

George Bird Grinnell

→────────────────────←

Edited, with Introduction and Commentary

by John F. Reiger

University of Oklahoma Press : Norman

Library of Congress Cataloging in Publication Data

Grinnell, George Bird, 1849-1938.
  The passing of the Great West.

  Reprint. Originally published: New York : Scribner, c1972.
  1. West (U.S.)—Description and travel—1860-1880—Addresses, essays, lectures. 2. West (U.S.)—History—1848-1950—Addresses, essays,
lectures. I. Reiger, John F. II. Title.
[F594.G77   1985]   .978'.02   84-19704
ISBN: 0-8061-1925-X

For my Mother and Father

From the foreword written by George Bird Grinnell in 1925 to the autobiography of Luther H. North, the famous scout:

"The men of the present day cannot conceive — because they have not had the experience to make them understand—the risks and . . . labors involved in that old wild life. So the old wild life can never be written of, except in the simple straightforward narrative of one of the quiet, modest men who had a part in it."

Contents

Introduction

During the nearly nine decades of his life, George Bird Grinnell (1849–1938) was an explorer, big-game hunter, rancher, naturalist, ethnologist, editor, author, and conservationist. He was a member of Othniel C. Marsh's geological expedition of 1870, which returned from the West with the best evidence up to that time of the validity of Darwin's theory of evolution. He was with Custer in the Black Hills in 1874 when the precious yellow ore was discovered, beginning one of the great gold rushes of American history. And in 1875, he accompanied Captain William Ludlow, of the Army's Corps of Engineers, on his reconnaissance of the Yellowstone region.

Grinnell journeyed beyond the Missouri in the last years of the Great West, a land typified by huge bison herds and free-ranging aborigines. While many others would travel in that wild country, Grinnell was unique. From a wealthy and influential family, he was able to meet men and afford trips outside the purview of the average individual. As a result, he experienced virtually every facet of Western life. Sensitive to the environment, he had a need to understand what he saw, and an unsurpassed education was the vehicle for satisfying that need. Finally, he possessed the aristocrat's dislike for change, a characteristic that compelled him to record his experiences in an effort to preserve — at least on paper — the life they represented.

Grinnell is best known today for his writings on the American Indian, which include scores of articles and a dozen books. After going through a number of editions during his lifetime, several of these volumes have recently been reprinted.

What makes his work so valuable is its authenticity. Grinnell *knew* the Plains Indians. He lived in their tepees for months at a time, in winter as well as summer. By the Pawnees, he was first known as "White Wolf," but later, after being adopted into the tribe, as "Pawnee Chief"; by the Blackfeet, he was known as "Fisher Hat," a name denoting great power; by the Gros Ventres, as "Gray Clothes," because of the way he was dressed when he first met them; and by the Cheyennes, as "Bird," because he came and went with the seasons like migratory waterfowl.[1]

The quality of Grinnell's writing on the Indian, particularly the Cheyenne, was not merely a product of time, but of his rare ability to step inside the skin of the red man. As Margaret Mead and Ruth Bunzel have observed in *The Golden Age of American Anthropology* (1960), Grinnell "knew and loved the prairie when the buffalo ran, before it had been torn up by plows and railroads. He loved the people of the prairie, too. And of all the tribes he knew, it was the Cheyenne he loved best. . . . Of . . . the books written about Indians, none comes closer to their everyday life than Grinnell's classic monograph on the Cheyenne. Reading it, one can smell the buffalo grass and the wood fires, [and] feel the heavy morning dew on the prairie."[2] Summarizing the conclusions of another noted scholar, Mari Sandoz, Grinnell's work on the Cheyenne is "the finest body of material on any American tribe . . . ."[3]

In addition to recording aboriginal history and culture, Grinnell fought to protect red men from the hostility of the surrounding white society. Using his personal contacts with politicians in Washington, D.C., and newspaper editors in New York City, he obtained food for the reservation Blackfeet of northwestern

Montana, who, before Grinnell was alerted, lost five hundred of their tribe to starvation during the winter of 1883–84; he led successful campaigns to oust corrupt or incompetent agents; and he helped Indians who had not been given the same rights as whites before the bar of justice.[4] When his friend, Theodore Roosevelt, ascended to the presidency in 1901, Grinnell drew upon his knowledge of Indian affairs to advise him. Among the services Grinnell performed for the President was the settling in 1902 of a national scandal involving a proposal to lease to cattlemen large sections of the Standing Rock Sioux Reservation on the border of North and South Dakota; the writing of parts of his 1902 and 1904 annual messages to Congress that dealt with Indians; and the suggesting of Francis E. Leupp for Commissioner of Indian Affairs, the man who filled that office with distinction during Roosevelt's second administration.[5]

Despite the association of Grinnell's name with ethnology and Indian reform, it was not in these fields but in conservation that he made his greatest impact on American history. In cataloguing his amazing array of accomplishments in a column-and-a-half obituary, the *New York Times* referred to him as the "father of American conservation."[6]

From his position as editor of *Forest and Stream*, the best outdoor journal of the 1880's and '90's, he consolidated the inchoate dissatisfaction among sportsmen with the rapid destruction of wildlife and habitat and channeled it into a crusade to husband natural resources. One outdoorsman in particular, Theodore Roosevelt, was impressed with Grinnell's views and incorporated them into his own philosophy.

In attempting to explain the origins of national conservation, historians have neglected the intellectual antecedents of Roosevelt's thought, the basis of the modern conservation program. Grinnell, the originator and amalgamator of ideas, *prepared* Roosevelt for Gifford Pinchot, the President's famous environmental administrator.

And Grinnell's career as an active conservationist did not end on Roosevelt's entry into the White House. Until 1929, when he was struck down by the first of a series of heart attacks, he continued to be an important figure in most of the environmental campaigns of his day. Often, he was even ahead of his time. With the present concern for conservation and ecology, it is worthy of note that he was protesting such "contemporary" problems as air and ocean pollution more than fifty years ago.[7]

Grinnell, like all men, was formed by the society of his early years. Though he loved the Great West and came to know it as intimately as any native, he preferred not to live there permanently. Ironically, he chose instead the highest product of the same civilization that was destroying it, New York City. In upbringing, culture, and sophistication, he was an Easterner, even an aristocrat, and nothing could change that. For this reason, his boyhood experiences in upper Manhattan are relevant to how he would later view the transformation of the Great West, and his memories of that period are included.

After Grinnell died, the bulk of his unpublished papers went to a friend, John P. Holman, who gave them to the Connecticut Audubon Society's Birdcraft Museum in Fairfield. Those papers, which were transferred to Yale University in 1984, are the basis of this book. Grinnell's "MEMOIRS," covering his life up to 1883, provide the chronology, and they are supplemented by excerpts from letters. Also included are selections from his published accounts of early Western trips, written for *Forest and Stream* in the 1870's and '80's. *The Passing of the Great West* is the preface to my *American Sportsmen and the Origins of Conservation* (New York, 1975), which focuses on the conservation achievements of Grinnell and his fellow sportsmen-naturalists in the period 1883–1901.

Because most of the present book is quoted material, I have dispensed with the usual custom of indenting long citations. Whenever possible, Grinnell is allowed to speak for himself, without the use of cumbersome phrases introducing his statements.

In pursuing my research I have acquired many obligations. I would like to thank the staffs of the New York Public Library, the Yale University Beinecke Rare Book and Manuscript Library, and the many photograph archives whose credits are listed with the picture in the book. Gratitude is due the late James B. Trefethen, Director of Publications of the Wildlife Management Institute, for aid in the location of sources. The late John P. Holman of Fairfield, Connecticut encouraged me to use the small number of Grinnell's papers in his own possession, as well as the huge collection he had given to the Connecticut Audubon Society before it was transferred to Yale. Of further help was the late Frank Novak, former curator of the Birdcraft Museum. Dr. Michael Davis was kind enough to read and comment on the manuscript. Most of all, I would like to thank my wife, Andrea, for her thoughtful suggestions and ceaseless encouragement.

1

Growing Up With
The Audubons

GEORGE BIRD GRINNELL was born in Brooklyn, New York, September 20, 1849, the oldest of five children of George Blake and Helen Alvord (Lansing) Grinnell. The family name was an old one in America, the first in the line being Matthew, a Huguenot from Burgundy, who arrived in what is now Rhode Island in 1630.[1] A number of Grinnell's ancestors had achieved fame and fortune. In the colonial period alone, if the lines of both his father and mother are combined, they include five governors and Betty Alden, one of the first white babies born in New England.[2]

Despite the venerable nature of the Grinnell name, the family had experienced periods of economic privation. One of the most difficult occurred during Grinnell's own adolescence. In the years before the Civil War, Grinnell's father was head of a New York textile firm that did most of its business with Southern planters. When war broke out the firm's customers were either unable, or unwilling, to pay their bills, and the company failed. Grinnell's father made a settlement with his creditors, promising eventually to pay the balance. Following peace, he became a stockbroker and

banker and improved his economic position so much that he was
able to retire from active business in 1873, when he was fifty.[3]

Unlike countless others, both North and South, who had been
hurt financially by the war and simply defaulted on their debts,
Grinnell's father thought it mandatory that unquestioned confidence in the family name be restored. In February, 1873, he not
only paid his creditors the balances owed but interest on the debts
as well, from the time of the settlement in 1861 up to 1873. His
son believed that "this was the first known occasion when a man
who had creditors had later paid these forgiven and often forgotten debts with interest on these debts. . . . I remember hearing at
the time that my father's action was commonly spoken of as something previously unheard of. . . ." The matter became well-known
in New York City financial circles even though the older Grinnell
"tried always to keep the matter quiet, and not to have anything
said about it."[4] The action of Grinnell's father reveals a firm, but
unobtrusive, commitment to financial probity. Assuming that this
uprightness was not limited to economic matters, its assimilation
by his son would help to explain the latter's self-effacing, yet
unrelenting, opposition to anyone who did not share his interpre-
tation of right conduct. In later years those who most often experienced Grinnell's wrath were the despoilers of the American
environment.

During his early childhood, Grinnell lived in several locations.
From Brooklyn, the first move was to Manhattan, when he was
four years old. The address was 96 West 21st Street, and as Grinnell recalled in his MEMOIRS, "this house stood west of Sixth
Avenue, for this was long before the system arose of numbering
the side streets in even hundreds between the avenues."[5] "During
our residence in West 21st Street, I was not large enough to
wander very far, but occasionally my father, who owned a fast
trotting horse which he drove in the morning before going to business, took me with him. . . . We drove out into 6th Avenue, and
as soon as 23rd Street was passed, we were on a dirt road on which
the horse could be driven at speed. This must have been about
1854 or 1855. It must have been just about this time that Central
Park was established, though for many years, little or nothing was
done in the way of its improvement. I can recall being taken out

one morning with my father and mother and some of their adult friends on a sleigh ride through Central Park. It was then a wilderness of rocks and pasture land."[6]

Grinnell also had a vivid memory of the site on which the original Madison Square Garden was later erected: "At this time Madison Square was a grass-grown, wholly unimproved lot surrounded by an old wooden fence that had once been painted brown. This was not of pickets, but had been an ornamental fence made of boards three or four inches wide, standing on end, separated, and ornamented on their edges by scroll work. Persons in the neighborhood of Madison Square who had goats used to drive them out to it to pasture, and I have a distinct mental picture of an old nannie with her head through a hole in the fence, watching the occasional passerby on 5th Avenue or Broadway as she chewed her cud."[7]

"It was very likely a question of the children's health that led my father to give up his house on 21st Street and move to the country. He hired at Weehawken [New Jersey] a place which belonged to Mr. Cossett, at that time a wealthy New York merchant.[8] The house stood on the very edge of the Palisades, adjoining Mr. Cossett's home place, and the view was superb. . . .

"It was in Weehawken that I first crossed [sat on] a horse, and was first thrown. There was a little piece of grass back of the house adjoining the garden in which Selim, my father's very gentle trotter, used to be turned for exercise. I succeeded one day in persuading the coachman, Amos Hovey, to put me on the animal's back where I sat for a little while in . . . fear and trembling. Amos, meantime, had gone off somewhere to his work, leaving me sitting on the horse. After I had become accustomed to my perch, riding seemed so easy that I wanted the horse to move. I managed to reach a twig of a tree, and breaking it off, struck the horse with it. He jumped and I rolled off, and was found . . . between his forelegs, while he investigated me with his nose.

"I think we remained only six months in Weehawken, but during that time there was a period of great cold (1856), and I used to believe that the Hudson River had frozen across. At all events, I know that my father walked out on it so far that he became a mere speck, and finally vanished from sight, but I cannot declare that he walked across." [9]

The most memorable hours of Grinnell's early childhood were spent at his grandfather's home in Greenfield, Massachusetts. Here was the large collection of mounted birds and mammals killed and preserved by his uncle, Thomas P. Grinnell. "Uncle Tom, who at that time must have been about twenty years of age, greatly impressed my youthful imagination by the stories that he told of hunting and fishing adventures, and by the pictures that he drew of birds. In his younger days he had made a large collection of mounted birds and mammals, which were in his father's house in Greenfield. Among these were what was said to be the last wild turkey killed on Mount Tom in Massachusetts in 1849, a raven killed in the same place, a deer killed near Greenfield, and a great number of birds large and small. In later years, and up to the time when I was twelve or fifteen years of age, I had no more pleasant hours, when at Greenfield, than those spent among Uncle Tom's birds in what was called the 'bird room.'"[10] Thus were sown the seeds of a lifetime fascination with the natural world and all it contained.

Grinnell was seven years of age when, on January 1st, 1857, his family moved to Audubon Park, the thirty acre, former estate of the famous naturalist. On Manhattan Island, between what is today 155th and 158th Streets, it was bordered on the east by the former Bloomingdale Road, now, roughly, Amsterdam Avenue, and on the west by the Hudson River. "George Blake Grinnell had set out from Weehawken early in the day alone, and a little later Mrs. Grinnell, with Hannah, the black nurse, carrying the baby and the three boys, drove to the Hoboken ferry and up north on New York Island. Amos, the coachman, drove the two bay horses, Selim and Emperor, to a closed carriage; on the seat by his side lay a little yellow dog that belonged to the stable, while Hector, the big white and black 'mastiff,' followed on foot. Snow was falling, and the Bloomingdale road was deep in mud and slush."[11] About a mile south of Audubon Park, on the Bloomingdale Road, lay the village of Manhattanville. Here, the party was delayed briefly, as "the horses were so tired that it was necessary to stop at a stable and procure another pair . . . ."[12] Finally, the Grinnells reached their destination, the home of Wellington Clapp, a wealthy dry-goods merchant who had leased his house to the family. They would live there for three years.

It was about 1860, then, as Grinnell recalled later, that "my father . . . purchased from Madam Audubon the old place in which I lived for more than half a century."[13] The house stood at what is today 157th Street, above Riverside Drive, almost on the exact spot where the "Riviera" apartment house has been erected. The "Grinnell" apartment house close by stands in what was once the family's cow pasture, while the entrance to the subway station on Broadway marks the former garden plot.[14]

It was to this section of upper Manhattan that John James Audubon had come to live in 1841, after finishing his multi-volume *Birds of America* (1827–38). In time other houses would be built in the area, including those of Audubon's two sons and Grinnell's father. Though never officially a park, the name "Audubon Park" quickly took hold of the imagination of New Yorkers and remained the common designation for the area until it was dismembered in 1909 by the expanding city.[15] When Grinnell was growing up, the tract was beautifully wooded, with groves of ancient chestnuts, oaks, and hemlocks, interspersed by a few country roads. The only settlement in the immediate vicinity was Carmansville. Then, "almost nothing was seen of what in later days was called 'improvement.' The fields and woods were left in a state of nature, and the different houses and their adjacent lands were not separated by barriers."[16] This fact, plus the presence of tame deer, elk, and other animals that roamed the area at will, made the tract very parklike indeed.

According to Grinnell, "It was while we still lived in the Clapp house that there occurred one autumn a tremendous flight of migrating robins. The ground was almost covered with them, and there seemed to be a robin to every square yard of ground. The birds were so many that it appeared impossible to throw a stone or shoot an arrow without killing one or more, and I armed myself with a hickory bow — purchased from the Indians at Saratoga and given me by Cousin George Bird — and two or three arrows, and started out to kill robins. Either there were fewer birds than I had supposed or I was not a good bowman, for I secured not one."[17]

It was also while Grinnell lived in the Clapp house that during one autumn morning before breakfast, his mother "saw that the dogwood tree which stood south of the circle was covered with passenger pigeons feeding on the berries. She dodged back into the hall, caught me by the arm, and brought me to the door where I could see them."[18] "There were so many . . . that all could not alight in it, and many kept fluttering about while others fed on the ground, eating the berries knocked off by those above."[19] "In later years there were regular autumnal flights of pigeons up and down the bank of the Hudson River until 1873 or 1874. We boys killed a few, shooting them from the roof."[20]

The passenger pigeon was once the most plentiful bird in America, and perhaps the world. While traveling through western Kentucky in the early 1800's, the naturalist, Alexander Wilson, witnessed an onrushing tide of pigeons that extended from horizon to horizon and took four hours to pass. The multitude darkened the sun and the roar of millions of wings almost deafened the human spectators. Some years later, Audubon visited a roost that was forty miles long; when its millions of occupants arrived at dark, the uproar could be heard over three miles away. When on their roosts, the birds were clubbed, netted and shot, and the great forests that sustained them were cut down. Still, who would have dreamed in Grinnell's youth that this species, once numbering in the *billions*, would not have one living representative today.[21]

While the Grinnell family was leasing the Clapp house, one of their son's best-liked play areas was "an old barn which may have been built by the naturalist for the accommodation of some of his wild animals." The building stood near Audubon's house, in what is now Riverside Drive. "It was a favorite place for climbing about by the small boys, and close up under its roof bats used to spend the day, and several were caught here during my investigations of the roof beams."[22]

Only rarely was the tranquility of Audubon Park disturbed. One such occasion was the Civil War draft riots. While they were going on, everyone in Grinnell's family except his father happened to be in Vermont. In the summer of 1863 the family returned to the "Hemlocks," as they called their new home, "but not until after the . . . riots were over. During these riots, the Hudson River Railroad did not run, and my father reached the house by crossing over to New Jersey, driving up to Fort Lee, and then being rowed across the river."[23]

In this period "the business part of New York [City] was well down town. The old Stewart store, the largest, best and perhaps most fashionable, retail dry goods store of that day, was at Chambers Street and Broadway. Delmonico's had a restaurant opposite Stewart's on the northwest corner of Broadway and Chambers Street. To reach the business part of the town from Audubon Park, it was necessary to take the Hudson River Railroad at the station called Carmansville — 152nd Street and North River. The train ran fast to about 30th Street and 10th Avenue, and from there more slowly down to the terminal at Chambers Street. Here the businessmen left it to go to their various offices and the shopping women left it to go to Broadway above . . . City Hall, where they made their purchases. On the other hand, in fine weather, many businessmen drove down, leaving their horses at some uptown livery stable, and then walked — or rode in the old-fashioned stages — down to the lower parts of the town.

"In those days the winters seemed more severe than at present; at least more snow fell, and as no attempt was made to clear it from the streets, it stayed longer on the ground. As soon as a heavy snow fall came, the high-wheel stages, drawn by two horses, were put aside, and low box sleighs on bobs took their places. The beds of these sleighs were full of straw, and people crowded in them sitting on seats at the sides. Two, four, or six horses, according to the depth of the snow, drew these sleighs swiftly. Boys and young men on the sidewalk sometimes snowballed the passengers, who protected themselves as well as they could by their coats and coat collars, and everybody was jolly and friendly. In fact, in those days, which now seem so long ago, a very considerable proportion of the men of any class in New York knew most of the other men in their class. All the dry goods merchants knew all the other dry goods merchants; all the businessmen down town were likely to have their watches cleaned, set and regulated by some particular man who had been long established in business . . . . New York at that time was not unlike a big country town; people lived simply and without pretense or airs."[24]

To the north, in Audubon Park, the life of the country was the dominant motif, as shown by the amusements of its children: "slidding [*sic*] down hill and skating in winter; swimming, crabbing, fishing, and picknicking in summer."[25] There were times, however, when these activities were superseded by ones not so harmless. In fact, Grinnell remembered "that the little boys of Audubon Park — all of them — ought to have been sent to some reform school, for they were bad, not perhaps judged by a boy's standard, but by that of an elderly man. They wanted excitement, and were determined to have it. . . . So they used to beat the pigs, steal chickens for surreptitious roasting at fires in the woods, occasionally steal figs, fruit, or anything edible from the village grocery store, steal food of any kind from their mother's pantry, steal cigars from their father, an offense which usually brought its own punishment, and one boy of this gang — I know of only one — stole a silver coin from a maid-servant's trunk to spend for the common good, and the other boys not actually guilty of the theft drank whatever it was that was purchased with the money without qualms of conscience.

"Most of the fathers of those boys were members of the volunteer fire department, and whenever a fire occurred and the boys knew of it, they too attended, 'running with the machine,' as it was then called. In time the boys succeeded in getting a pair of wheels, fastened a tongue to the axle and, getting some old rubber hose, they made a hose cart of their own, with which now they attended fires with a feeling of greatly added dignity. The mothers of most of them provided them with red shirts and some even had a genuine fireman's helmet. This must have been about 1860 to 1861."[26]

When Grinnell's family moved to Audubon Park, the Hudson River Railroad had already been operating for about seven years. When constructed, "the line was made as straight as possible, and the road was built in part on an embankment thrown up at some distance from the shore of the river and running from one point on the bank to another. Thus, from what is now 155th Street up to about 180th Street, there existed a succession of small ponds . . . which lay between the old shore of the river and the embankment on which the railroad ran. Culverts through this embankment gave passage to the river water as the tide ebbed and flowed. The ponds were muddy on bottom and were resorted to by small fish and crabs, which the small boys — and sometimes their parents — caught at the proper season, while in winter the frozen ponds furnished skating grounds for old and young. . . . When the weather was not cold enough to freeze the saline water of the river, neighboring ponds were resorted to, one of which was on the old Field farm, just about where Broadway now runs, perhaps at 147th Street. Another was Swackhammer's pond which lay north of what is [presently] . . . 175th Street, and west of what is now 10th Avenue, not far from where the New York Juvenile Asylum stood for so many years.

"Besides the Hudson River Railroad, which was the usual means of reaching the city, as it was then spoken of, the only other public transportation line was a stage which started from Saul's tavern, at the corner of 162nd Street and the Bloomingdale Road, and went down to 36th Street and Broadway, the journey taking about one and one-half hours. . . . Usually the women of the different families, when they went to New York to make extensive shopping tours or to call, drove down, following the Bloomingdale Road down to what was called Breakneck Hill, which was about midway between what is now St. Nicholas Avenue and 8th Avenue, below the present 145th Street. Breakneck Hill was a very steep descent, with sharp turns, over and between rocky ledges, where, presumably, at some time a broken harness or runaway horses had caused the wreck of a carriage or wagon."[27]

"In those days none of the modern streets had been opened, though 155th Street was a country lane leading down to Audubon Park, and 158th Street was another, by which teams reached the 'sugar house,'" the name the local inhabitants had given to the sugar refinery which stood on the river bank near the foot of 160th Street.[28] "The line of 156th Street from Audubon Park to Bloomingdale Road was not crossed by fences. A brook flowed down through it, and two or three shanties, occupied by laboring men, stood in what was later the street, but there was a path along the brook leading from the Park to the village, which people might follow to save going around two corners, if their business led them directly east.

"The village was Carmansville, a collection of· two dozen houses on both sides of the Bloomingdale Road. There was one butcher shop, two grocery stores, a drug store, and up at the forks of the road, where the Bloomingdale and Kingsbridge Roads crossed, there was a blacksmith shop. . . .

"South of Audubon Park, on the river bank, and west of the tracks of the railroad, stood the blast furnace. . . . This was an ancient pile of brick, where iron ore brought . . . by water was smelted into pigs. The molten iron was blown off twice a day, at noon and at midnight, and occasionally the neighbors went down to see the night blast and took their children with them. The small boys, if by any chance they could get away at night or by day, delighted to go down to the foundry, as they called it, both to see the molten iron running from the furnace and also to play on the schooners that brought the ore. . . . Nevertheless, this was forbidden ground, and boys were very much afraid of the workmen, so that the place was not greatly frequented.

"One of the chief summer amusements of the boys of Audubon Park was swimming in the river. There were various places outside of the railroad embankment where the sand beach came to the surface and where those who did not know how to swim might bathe safely. Such a place was halfway between Carmansville station and the foundry; another immediately south of Carmansville station; another was halfway between 152nd Street and 155th Street, and one again between 155th and 158th Street. These beaches also were great places for soft clams and occasionally a few of these were dug by the small boys and carried home. The older boys who knew how to swim frequented some of the various docks, where they used to dive into the water from the tops of the high spiles, much as small boys do everywhere. About 1861 or 1862, . . . people passing uptown in the Hudson River trains, being offended by the sight of the naked children dancing on top of the spiles and . . . making an exhibition of themselves, complained of the practice, and an ordinance was passed that no bathing should be done unless the bather wore tights. The ordinance was little regarded, but on one occasion when a train passed south, a policeman riding in it saw Paul Ferguson and myself in swimming at the 158th Street dock, and leaving the train at 152nd Street, came back and arrested us for violation of the ordinance.

"We were . . . alarmed and depressed by the situation. The policeman walked with us up to Tubby Hook, about two miles, where we were locked in a cell in the police station, a small wooden building which stood on the south side of the Kingsbridge Road. . . . An hour or two of this confinement gave us plenty of time to ponder on the surprises and sorrows of life. After a time we were brought from the cell, ordered to step into a licensed vender's wagon, which the police had borrowed or taken, and with the complaining policeman were driven down to Jefferson Market Police Court, which . . . was at the corner of 8th Street and 6th Avenue. It was a ramshackle building. The presiding justice was Judge Quackenbush. As I recall it, there was no special business before the court, and we were at once hustled to the bar of justice. We were both so short that the Judge in looking at the prisoners was obliged to rise to his feet, rest his hands on his desk, and bend over to look down on them.

"The Judge asked the officer what the complaint was, and when it was explained, he ordered the policeman to take those children back to their mothers without delay, and declared that he ought to be ashamed of himself for having brought them to court. We were much relieved when we started on our drive back to Carmansville, and fuming with indignation at the policeman who had . . . been put in the wrong by the justice. As we reached Breakneck Hill on our return, we met Captain Wilson, the local captain of police, driving to the city in search of us. He had learned only a short time before of what had happened and hurried down to bring the boys back to their parents.

"In the year 1860, Albert Edward, then Prince of Wales, and afterward King of England, came to America and spent some time in New York. His arrival created great excitement. A ball was given for him, and . . . my mother attended it.

"Some time before this my father had given me a pony. The little animal was brought up one summer afternoon and having been saddled and bridled, I was put on it, feeling considerable trepidation. When the person holding it let go the bridle, for some reason . . . the beast bolted and running under the low branches of a hemlock tree close to the saddle, I was swept off, the saddle turning at the same time.

"When the pony was caught, my father tied two or three knots in the saddle girth, put on and tightened the saddle properly, and obliged me to remount and ride off. I soon became more or less at home on the little horse, and soon learned that to be thrown involves no great hardship. I must have ridden altogether by balance, and without holding on at all with my legs, for the pony had a trick of galloping along at a good rate, and stopping suddenly, and I invariably turned a summersault over his head and alighted on my back in the road. Sometimes the wind was knocked out of me for a little while, but nothing serious ever occurred.

"During the visit of the Prince of Wales, one afternoon while riding, I was overtaken by a carriage accompanied by several policemen on horseback, which contained Mayor Wood and a young man in a red coat whom I at once knew must be the Prince of Wales. I galloped my pony for a little way along the side of the road by the carriage and took off my cap, and the Prince of Wales waved his cap at me with a friendly grin."[29]

"It must have been 1860 . . . or 1861, when I was eleven or twelve years old, that I first began to go shooting. These early efforts were made secretly in company with Harry Clapp, the oldest son of Wellington Clapp, who had returned to Audubon Park, to the house my father had occupied for about three years. They were made secretly, because we supposed that our parents would forbid our use of firearms if they knew of it. Tom Harden, the village tailor, a cripple, owned a British military musket of considerable size and weight, which, as a great favor, he would sometimes lend us. We purchased powder, shot and caps at a store in the village, . . . and carrying the ammunition in bottles in our pockets, in the traditional small boy way, we used to steal off through the fields northward to Harris' woods between 158th and 162nd Streets, west of what is now Broadway, and through the woods northward as far as Tubby Hook. Small birds were the game pursued: meadowlarks, robins, golden-winged woodpeckers and occasionally a wild pigeon. In these woods there were many dogwood trees, and in autumn when the berries were ripe,

migrating birds resorted to them in numbers. We used to hide
near such trees and shoot the birds. The musket was far taller
than either boy, and so heavy that unaided, neither could hold
it to the shoulder. It was the practice to take alternate shots, one
boy standing or sitting in front of the other and allowing the
shooter to rest the barrel of the gun on his shoulder. When the
gun was to be reloaded, it was necessary to hold it very much
off the perpendicular; otherwise, we could not have put the
charge in the barrel or rammed it down with the steel ramrod.
The caps used were the now forgotten 'hat caps' which were
shaped somewhat like a high hat, the copper spread all about the
opening which contained the fulminate. Eley caps had already
been invented and were in common use, but we did not know
of them, and if we had, we could not have found any large enough
to fit the nipple of the musket. Some time after that, on an occasion when Tom Harden declined to loan us the musket, we
borrowed from William Cameron, then station agent for the
Hudson River Railroad at 152nd Street, a light and more or less
modern — for those times — single-barrel shotgun which we used
with great joy and success. Gradually, we extended our wander-
ings further afield and used to go up to Dykeman's meadows on
the Harlem River, where peeps, small sandpipers and small
herons were sometimes to be had, and at rare intervals a duck
was seen.

"It was perhaps a year or two later that my Uncle Will — possibly learning of my excursions, or having heard me talk about
shooting — presented me with a light double-barrel gun, which
I used thereafter with the consent of my parents. . . . After this,
we used to go shooting up to Van Cortlandt Lake, then called
Bronson's, and here on a number of occasions were seen flocks
of quail and . . . snipe. Here too was a fish hawk's nest in a tall
tree on the hill northeast of the lake.[30] The hill is now part of
Van Cortlandt Park.

"About this time, too, a woodcock one autumn made its appearance in our garden, near what would now be the corner of
157th Street and Broadway, and until forced to migrate, it gave
me abundant shooting. Every morning before breakfast, I sallied
out, put up the bird, and shot at it. Often I found it again, later
in the day. I never hit it, but it gave me much excitement.

"At that time, and for many years afterward, there was a large swamp west of 10th Avenue, south of 175th Street, and east of the Bloomingdale Road, which was a favorite resort for the boys with whom I associated. Green herons bred in the swamp, and from this fact we called it the Green Heron Woods. Woodcock also bred there and were occasionally seen and shot at. South of the Green Heron Woods was pasture land interrupted by occasional old stone walls, and copses of undergrowth to the point where 10th Avenue and Kingsbridge Roads come together. I recall but one house in this triangle, which must have been three quarters of a mile long, and this was the old stone Cross Keys Tavern. There was a tradition that Washington had once slept there, and in my youth there still swung from a beam projecting out toward the road, west, a large weatherbeaten sign, on which was painted the two long keys crossing each other, which gave the house its name. I cannot recall that it was ever used as a tavern. In my day it was occupied by one or two Irish families, whose pigs, hens, ducks and dogs were always to be seen on the borders of the puddles that stood at the sides of the house.

"In what used to be called the Blind Asylum Woods, on the steep side hill above the Deaf and Dumb Asylum, I . . . once startled a ruffed grouse from under a tree. This would be on the east side of the present Riverside Drive, perhaps about 165th Street. In those woods cottontail rabbits used to be plenty, and in autumn many ducks and geese were to be seen flying up or down the river. On more than one occasion, a flock of quail was seen in autumn in Audubon Park."[31]

A much more common visitor to the area was the American symbol, the bald eagle. "In winter the river was often very full of ice, and eagles and crows were constantly seen walking about on the ice, no doubt feeding on refuse and the bodies of animals thrown into the stream further north. The crows used to roost on a cedar-covered knoll north of the Harlem River in what is now the Bronx, not very far from Highbridge, and each morning they flew across the island to the ice in the river. In foggy or stormy weather they flew low — among the tree tops. Sometimes the eagles would alight on the trees not far from the house, and I recall one occasion of much excitement when three eagles, one carrying a fish, and the others pursuing him, came close to the house, and alighted on a white oak tree in front of it. They were quarreling and fighting for the prize, which the captor at last dropped and which when brought to the house proved to be a barbel, weighing a pound or more."[32] The bald eagle is a species that does not appreciate human company, and its abundance is proof of the wildness of upper Manhattan during Grinnell's childhood. The eagles have long since gone, and the river they fished in is now so polluted that much of its former life has vanished; the eagle itself is threatened with extinction.

One of Grinnell's favorite winter activities took place in the company of John James Audubon's oldest grandson: "Jack Audubon ... was privileged by his father to carry his grandfather's gun on many shooting excursions, and I often went with him in winter over to the Harlem River to see him shoot muskrats. At that time an arm of the Harlem River ran south through where the Polo Grounds now are, as far as the present 145th Street west of 8th Avenue; but there was a tongue of solid land east of this running up to Macomb's Dam Bridge. In other words, the land where the elevated railroad now runs — 8th Avenue — was then above the reach of the tide. Across this tidewater flat — in a general way about where the Viaduct, 155th Street, now runs — was a footbridge. A footpath ran ... down the hill near where 155th Street is, and a little south of it, and when the water's edge was reached, one stepped onto a narrow bridge, two planks wide, the planks resting on poles driven into the mud of the bottom. There were many muskrats in this water, and after it froze up in winter, they resorted to certain holes in the ice where we watched for them. They were not often killed, but occasionally Jack got one and much more often thought that he had killed one which he could not recover.

"It was after I got my gun that with Jack Audubon, Harry Clapp and one or two other boys, I went across the river and camped under the Palisades, sleeping out-of-doors for the first time. We carried with us some food, for it is doubtful if any of us knew how to make a fire, much less cook. We slept on the ground, and ... it rained during the night, and in the morning the barrels of my gun, which I had stood up against a tree, had a lot of water in them. On the way across the river, either going or coming, Jack Audubon shot a little duck. . . . It was probably a blue-winged teal.

"In those days Eighth Avenue and Harlem Lane were dirt roads where men who owned trotting horses came to exercise their animals and to trot them against each other. Close to Macomb's Dam was a hotel . . .,and on the piazza . . . the drivers, [after] putting their horses under the sheds of the hotel, sat and smoked and watched other people drive."[33] Grinnell's father and his business associate, Cornelius ["Commodore"] Vanderbilt, were two of these men.

"In the meadows west of 8th Avenue about 140th Street were occasional small marshy places where cattails grew and the red-wing blackbirds had their nests. South of what is now 125th Street were truck farms usually carried on by thrifty Germans."[34]

When the Grinnell family first moved to Audubon Park, "the naturalist Audubon had been dead about six years, but his sons Victor and John Woodhouse Audubon were still carrying on his studies. . . . Victor Audubon at that time was bedridden, owing to a fall, but John Woodhouse was an extraordinarily active man of great energy. He was constantly receiving natural history specimens from correspondents all over North America and painting the specimens that he received. He had three sons, Jack, Billy and Ben. Victor had only one son, Gifford. . . .

"The widow of the naturalist lived with her oldest son. She had apparently no means, though she had much land."[35] But much of the land was then unsalable. "I have a vivid memory of an occasion when my father took me with him when he went to see [her] . . . to conclude the purchase of a piece of land, and of the great relief, satisfaction, and even gratitude, that she expressed to him for his willingness to make the purchase. The scene touched me, even though for years afterward I did not understand its meaning."[36]

The reason for the widow's financial plight was that "her sons were in no sense moneymakers, and had no notion whatever of the value of money. Madame Audubon, or 'Grandma' Audubon, as all the children called her, seemed to be doing for her sons and their families something like what she had been doing for her husband during much of the time since their marriage — earning the bread for the family. To do this, she had a school, whose quarters were in her bedroom. . . ."[37] This was located "in the southeast room of the second story of the Victor Audubon house."[38] The neighborhood children, as well as her own grandchildren, attended the school, and it was here that Grinnell learned the fundamentals of arithmetic.

Grandma Audubon "was a beautiful, white-haired old lady with extraordinary poise and dignity; most kindly and patient and affectionate, but a strict disciplinarian of whom all the children stood in awe."[39] " 'She loved to read, to study, and to teach. She knew how to gain the attention of the young, and to fix knowledge in their minds.' "[40]

Of the individuals who helped shape Grinnell's early interest in natural history, none was as important as Audubon's widow. Whether her instruction was given in a formal, or, as was more common, informal situation, it had an enduring effect on his life. Years later, when he founded the first Audubon Society, he named it as much for her as for her husband. In fact, he believed that she was responsible for Audubon's success. Before meeting her, Audubon lacked the purpose and discipline to capitalize on his talent. "The great lesson of his [Audubon's] life lies in our recognition . . . that he triumphed in the strength of another, who moulded his character, shaped his aims, gave substance to his dreams, and finally, by the exercise of that self-denial which he was incapable of as a long-sustained effort, won for him the public recognition and reward of his splendid talents."[41]

Grandma Audubon affirmed repeatedly that self-denial was the key to success in life. Because Grinnell's morally upright father had prepared him for this idea, a commitment to its practice became part of the boy's personality. In later reform campaigns, Grinnell often emphasized the need for self-sacrifice. When, for example, he spearheaded a movement for the preservation of American waterfowl, he argued that only self-denial on the part of hunters — imposing bag limits on themselves and eliminating shooting in the spring — would save the ducks and geese.

When Grinnell thought of his childhood, Grandma was always at the center of the recollection. Their relationship is typified by the following: "One morning in late winter or early spring, on my way to school, I had almost reached the Victor Audubon house when I saw a dozen or twenty small greenish birds feeding on the grass under a pine tree. I approached them slowly, trying to see what they were; and they did not fly, even when I was within a few feet of them. I did not know them, and they were so tame that I resolved to try to catch one. The crab net used in summer always hung in the area under the Victor Audubon piazza, and backing away from the birds I ran there, secured the net, and returned. It was not difficult for a cautious lad to get near enough to the little birds to pass the net over one, and when I had caught it I rushed into the house and up to Grandma's room, and showed her my prize. She told me that the bird was a Red Crossbill — a young one — pointed out the peculiarities of the bill, told me something about the bird's life, and later showed me a picture of it. Then after a little talk she and I went downstairs and out-of-doors, found the birds still feeding there, and set the captive free."[42]

The sons of John James Audubon also helped to build in Grinnell a fascination with the outdoors. "The houses occupied by Victor and John Woodhouse Audubon were interesting because they were so full of material pertaining to the great naturalist. On the walls were the antlers of deer and elk, supporting rifles and shotguns, . . . powder horns and shot, and ball pouches. There were many trophies from the Missouri River, a region which in those days seemed infinitely remote and romantic with its tales of trappers, trading posts and Indians. Paintings of birds and animals adorned the walls of the rooms, many from the brush of John James Audubon and others from those of his sons or . . . his assistants. I remember particularly the painting of pheasants and spaniels, . . . the painting of the eagle and the lamb, . . . and two or three portraits of the naturalist, at least one of them by himself."[43]

But of these, the huge eagle and lamb picture was Grinnell's favorite. "I greatly admired it and often talked about it to Grandma Audubon, and on one occasion she told me that after her death the picture should be mine. Boylike, I treasured this memory, but the promise was not again referred to."[44] After her death, however, Grandma's will showed that she had not forgotten the pledge. The valuable painting was left to Grinnell, and it hung in a prominent place in his home throughout his life.[45]

During his childhood in the Park, Grinnell's favorite play area was the loft of the barn belonging to Audubon's younger son. Piled against the walls were the red, muslin-bound ornithological biographies, as well as boxes of bird skins collected on the naturalist's expeditions. "John Woodhouse Audubon was in constant communication with various naturalists, and frequently received boxes of fresh specimens, around which, while they were being opened, the boys [from the neighborhood] gathered to wonder at the strange animals that were revealed."[46] Audubon's older son, Victor, was also active in ornithological work for many years after his father's death. Together, the two men continually reinforced Grinnell's growing enthusiasm for all things pertaining to the natural world.

As Grinnell grew older, his intimate association with the Audubon family naturally led him to read Audubon's descriptions of his wilderness travels. Of particular interest to the boy was the naturalist's account of his last expedition, made in 1843. Setting out from his home in the Park — merely a stone's throw down the hill from the future site of the Grinnell house — Audubon ascended the Missouri and Yellowstone Rivers. In describing the countless herds of buffalo encountered, and their slaughter, he wrote: "What a terrible destruction of life, as it were for nothing, . . . as the tongues only were brought in, and the flesh of these fine animals was left to beasts and birds of prey, or to rot on the spots where they fell. The prairies are literally *covered* with the skulls of the victims. . . ." But Audubon knew that "this cannot last; even now there is a perceptible difference in the size of the herds, and before many years the Buffalo, like the Great Auk, will have disappeared; surely this should not be permitted."[47] His nearly accurate prediction was remarkable for the time; over twenty years later, at the close of the Civil War, there were still millions of bison on the Great Plains. Few men in Audubon's time, or even in the early years of Grinnell's Western expeditions, believed that the numberless buffalo could be reduced by century's end to a mere remnant, tottering on the brink of extinction.

A generation after Audubon had set out for the West, Grinnell would follow. Once again, the inhabitants of the Park would be vibrant with enthusiasm over the adventure that was about to befall one of their number. Even Grandma Audubon lived long enough to witness the preparation for two of Grinnell's expeditions. In 1875, just a year after she died, a third trip traced the same route her husband had taken in 1843. Grinnell, too, found incredible slaughter taking place throughout the upper Missouri region. Not only buffalo but all the larger mammal species were being wantonly destroyed. As noted in a subsequent chapter, he included in the government report of the expedition one of the first official protests against the excessive killing of Western big game. This was the formal beginning of his career as a conservationist. Audubon's 1843 account of the white man's treatment of the bison probably played its part in Grinnell's decision to submit the protest. Essentially, the latter was an elaboration of Audubon's warning about the possible extinction of the buffalo: "Surely this should not be permitted."

Although Grinnell's childhood years were shaped most by certain persons — his father, his uncle, and the Audubon family — their effect on him probably would have been quite different in dissimilar surroundings. The spark of enthusiasm for nature kindled by his uncle might well have died out in the middle of a large city. But in the beautiful countryside of the Park, it became a fire, fed by the ceaseless encouragement of the Audubons. Perhaps if Grinnell had spent most of his youthful years in a metropolis, his keen ethical sense inherited from his father would later have turned him to urban reform. Instead, he wedded his code of justice to his love of nature. Unlike Audubon, who had observed and only lamented, Grinnell would observe, lament — and fight — carrying on his crusade until the problem was either eliminated or it was obvious that he was utterly beaten. There were, however, few of the latter experiences. Practically all the movements that he started, or helped to start, were eventually successful.

Not all of Grinnell's childhood hours were spent in outdoor pastimes, but his affinity for these activities kept him from pursuing his formal education with anything approaching dedication. In his early years in the Park he had been tutored, along with a few other neighborhood children, by Audubon's widow. Later, in the fall of 1861, he "was sent to the French Institute, which stood in a large, old, country place on land now built over, about 170th Street, west of the present Broadway. . . . The building was a large old-fashioned house. . . . It burned down many years ago. All the instructors were French or Spanish. . . . One of the teachers was reported to have been a soldier under Napoleon and to have been in the retreat from Moscow. He looked the part, for he was tall, slim, erect, and wore a fierce moustache and imperial. The students here were a few Americans, a few French and a larger number of Mexican, Cuban and South American lads, perhaps forty or fifty in all. . . . They were a harum-scarum lot . . . who played very hard and studied not at all, making all sorts of fun of two or three instructors; but they were in deadly terror of the Spanish teacher and the old Napoleonic soldier, who in enforcing order used only their eyes."[48]

After Grinnell had attended the French Institute for two years, his parents decided that it was time to place their son in a more disciplined environment. They chose, therefore, to send him to Churchill Military School in what is now Ossining, New York, north of New York City on the Hudson. It was the fall of 1863 and Grinnell's fourteenth birthday. Because he has left no record of how he felt upon leaving home for the first time, his feelings can only be guessed at. It is likely, however, that he experienced the same ambivalence countless boys have felt since in similar situations: anticipation of adventure on one hand and a sense of foreboding on the other. The chance to explore a new and wilder section of his beloved Hudson must certainly have appealed to him; but this was counterbalanced by anxiety at leaving his parents and Audubon Park and the realization that harder work and an almost constant demand for self-discipline would be imposed on him. He quickly rose to the challenge of the military routine, however, and even flourished in this area of the curriculum. "I started in as a small boy as a private in the rear rank, and finally got to be an officer in command of the company."[49]

It was while Grinnell was attending Churchill that Abraham Lincoln was shot. "This took place during a Spring vacation. The same morning I went down to New York [City] with my mother and still remember the air of gloom that pervaded the whole city, the eagerness with which people purchased fresh editions of the newspapers, and the tears which rolled down the faces of women, and even of some men, as they walked along the streets. No one old enough to observe, and in New York at that time, can forget that day. . . .

"My father took me to the City Hall where Mr. Lincoln lay in state, and on that occasion I had pointed out to me a number of well-known men of the day, especially soldiers who had been in command of large bodies of troops during the war. I do not recall the names of these people, except that of General [Ambrose Everett] Burnside."[50]

While at Churchill, Grinnell excelled in drill and other military activities, but as usual he did poorly in academic matters. Nevertheless, his father was determined that he should follow the family tradition by going to Yale. Realizing that he had "wasted" his time at Churchill, Grinnell had no intention of going on to college. "I did not in the least wish to go, and tried to escape it, but my parents had made up their minds, and I was not in the habit of questioning my father's decisions."[51]

Since he had no other choice, Grinnell decided to make a titanic effort to pass his entrance examinations. The head of the military school assured him this was impossible. But after graduating in 1866, he spent the whole summer trying to make up for what he should have learned during the school year. "I did work hard, but with no special intelligence, for I had never learned how to study. I was usually called early in the morning, studied Latin and Greek until breakfast, and spent the morning, afternoon and evening doing the same thing."[52] His tutors were the best; one was William Graham Sumner, just beginning his teaching career at Yale. "The vacation passed, and in September I went to New Haven with my father, and was examined. By good fortune I managed to get through, though I had conditions in Greek and in Euclid."[53]

The first year at Yale was uneventful, possibly because he was too frightened of the older boys and of failing his academic work to get into trouble. With the beginning of sophomore year, he manifested a new confidence. "Barely seventeen years old, and quite without any sense of responsibility, I was perpetually in trouble."[54] He "took part in all the [freshman] hazing and hat-stealing which was usual by Sophomores at that epoch. Aided and abetted by two classmates, . . . one stormy night I climbed the lightning rod on the building known as the Lyceum, and with red paint inscribed the number of the class on the face of the college clock. There it remained one or two days, to the enormous pride of my class, until the college carpenter was able to devise a means of getting up to the clock face and erasing it."[55] The inevitable clash with authority finally arrived when he was seen hazing a freshman and suspended for one year. With a companion, he was sent to Farmington, Connecticut, to be tutored by Reverend L. R. Payne, pastor, ironically, of the same church once presided over by one of Grinnell's ancestors.[56]

Instead of punishment, the time spent at Farmington proved to be a kind of extended vacation. "We had a very good time, doing very little studying, and spending most of our time out-of-doors. We took long walks, paddled on the Farmington River, and on moonlight nights in winter used to spend pretty much all night tramping over the fields.

"At the end of the year the college authorities permitted us to return to New Haven and pass our examinations with the class. My idleness at Farmington resulted in a failure to pass . . . , but I received permission to try again. The next Autumn, which was the beginning of my Junior year, I went to Stamford, Connecticut, . . . and was tutored by Dr. Hurlburt, one of the dearest of men, for whom I always had a strong affection. Dr. Hurlburt was not only a good tutor, but a good handler of boys. He got me a boarding place, not very far from his house, and every morning used to have me out of bed by seven. While making his rounds, he took me with him in his chaise, heard me recite as we drove along, and made me study while he was paying his professional calls. This . . . continued for two terms, or until the end of the Spring vacation, when I returned to college and passed my examinations with flying colors. That I did so was not at all to my credit, but was wholly due to Dr. Hurlburt."[57]

The rest of Grinnell's junior year was a little better than his first two, and perhaps as a reward, his parents took him on a three month tour of England, Scotland, France, and Switzerland. But on returning to Yale, he immediately reverted to his old ways.

While he received his B.A. in 1870, on schedule, he recalled that "I was in great fear lest my degree should be withheld on account of my poor scholarship."[58]

Because of Grinnell's inferior record, it would have probably seemed incredible to his teachers and classmates if they had known then that he would return to Yale and receive a Ph.D. in 1880 and an honorary Lit.D. in 1921. His future career would reveal an ability for ceaseless work, great physical and intellectual discipline, and a rare aptitude for exact observation. Why, then, were none of these traits evident in his undergraduate days? The most probable answer is that he was in temporary rebellion against his parents, especially his father, for imposing on him four years of college he never wanted. Later, when he himself decided that he would pursue graduate studies, the underlying traits were revealed.

In the year Grinnell entered Yale the college awarded Othniel C. Marsh the first chair of paleontology in the United States. Four years later, this appointment would transform Grinnell's life. In the summer of 1868 Marsh had found fossil bones of an extinct horse, scarcely a yard long, at Antelope Station, Nebraska. Besides adding key support to the theory of evolution, the find convinced him that the West was a great, untapped reservoir of fossil remains; immediately he began planning an expedition.[59] "Toward the close of the Senior year it was reported that Professor O. C. Marsh, who was not an instructor, and was known to the undergraduates only by sight, purposed that summer to lead a scientific expedition to the West. . . . This rumor greatly interested me, for I had been brought up, so to speak, on the writings of Captain Mayne Reid, which dealt with travel on the plains, and among the mountains, between 1840 and 1850. His stories had appealed to my imagination, and I had always been eager to visit the scenes he described, but had supposed that they were far beyond my reach. When, however, I heard of this proposed expedition, and learned too that the party would . . . be made up from recent graduates of the college, I determined that I must try to be one of these. After several days' consideration, I at last summoned up courage to call on Professor Marsh, and tell him what I desired. He discouraged me at our first interview, but said that he would inquire about me and at a second meeting seemed more favorably· disposed. A little later he accepted me as a volunteer. After . . . that, he asked my advice about the constitution of his party, and I very naturally recommended a number of men I knew well, who would be likely to be useful to him and agreeable to me. Among these were John R. Nicholson, long chancellor of the state of Delaware; John W. Griswold, of Troy, New York; and James M. Russell, of Kentucky."[60]

Why Marsh acted as he did, knowing of Grinnell's inferior performance at Yale, is difficult to fathom. Perhaps it was the latter's unbounded enthusiasm that carried the day, or the favorable report of an unknown supporter. In any case, it *is* known that from the time these two men began working together their relationship was completely harmonious. In fact, of all Marsh's assistants, Grinnell became his favorite.[61]

The paleontologist and his twelve helpers left New Haven on June 30, 1870, "bound for a West that was then really wild and woolly."[62] "Probably none of them except the leader had any motive for going other than the hope of adventure with wild game or wild Indians."[63]

2

Rediscovering
The West

ACCORDING TO HISTORIAN William H. Goetzmann, Marsh's expedition marked a new trend in exploration of the West. It was the first of a series of annual trips made from 1870 to 1873, financed mostly by Marsh's own funds and composed, with the exception of himself, of Yale volunteers — students and recent graduates. Though the country they investigated was often unmapped and in the hands of hostile Indians, they were not "discoverers" in the most common sense of the word; one or more military surveys had already penetrated the regions. Nevertheless, these men were true explorers whose discoveries were more subtle than the finding of a previously unknown mountain or valley, but easily as important. With the perspective of a new science, they went West destined to make new kinds of disclosures, sometimes in areas traversed many times before. There is no better example than Marsh's find at Antelope Station, where his professional training, acquired at Yale's Sheffield Scientific School and in Germany, enabled him to detect something priceless in what others would have regarded only as refuse. The success of Marsh's expeditions and their essentially civilian character "made it clear that the days of the pure military reconnaissance were rapidly passing . . . . The emphasis had shifted to a more sophisticated approach to Western exploration. But though this phase of its activities had been curtailed, the Army played a great role for a time in developing the newer, more sophisticated academic approaches to scientific exploration in the West."[1]

The plan of the Marsh expedition was to follow the recently completed transcontinental railroad, taking extended side trips north and south of the line.[2] The railroad officials went out of their way to aid the party, even to the point of lowering or eliminating fares.[3]

The journey through the settled portions of the country was uneventful, but as they neared Omaha, their excitement grew. The town was on the edge of the back country; one hundred miles west was the land of the Sioux and the Cheyenne. To cross the Missouri from Council Bluffs, the group boarded a stern-wheel steamer. As Grinnell recalled in his autobiography, "I was fascinated by the appearance of one of the passengers, who carried a long rifle and wore moccasins. I believed that now I was on the frontier, and I was not far wrong."[4]

The party stayed several days in Omaha where one of the main activities was zeroing in their Henry rifles. Since most had not fired their weapons before, they set up targets on the prairie in what is now downtown Omaha and banged away.[5] The marksmanship was little better than dismal, but after some practice it was decided that the group now had at least a chance of survival if attacked by aborigines.

Leaving the Missouri, the expedition again headed west. In eastern Nebraska the train was stopped twice because buffalo blocked the tracks. The first delay was short, so the second time this happened "we supposed they would soon pass by, but they kept coming. . . ."[6] It was only then that Grinnell realized that the animals were "in numbers so great that they could not be computed. . . ."[7] Three hours later, the last buffalo crossed in front of the train.

Finally, the party reached its first jumping-off spot, Fort McPherson, located about sixteen miles east of the forks of the Platte

River, near the present town of Maxwell. William F. ("Buffalo Bill") Cody was the post's chief scout.

"He was a tall, well-built, handsome man who wore his blonde hair long and was a striking figure; above all on horseback. Like many outdoor men on the plains and in the mountains in those early days, he wore buckskin clothing . . . , and in such dress Cody's splendid physique made him very noticeable. . . . Shooting from the ground with a rifle, Cody was a very ordinary shot, . . . but he was the finest horseback rifle shot ever known. . . . His skill in killing buffalo, on the run, no doubt gave him his common name. . . . In the year 1870 he performed a most remarkable feat, when in riding after buffalo, he killed sixteen in sixteen shots."[8]

The day the Marsh expedition arrived at Fort McPherson, "two or three antelope hunters who had been out from the post were attacked by a small party of Indians, and one of them received an arrow through the arm, but shot the boy who used the bow. When the hunters reached the post, a force of troops, with Cody, was sent out to follow the Indians. They did not find them, except the body of the boy Johnny Wetzel [the hunter] had shot. He was wrapped in his buffalo robe, and lay on a hill only a mile or two beyond where his wound was received. His moccasins and other apparel showed that he was a Cheyenne."[9] To the twenty-year-old Grinnell looking down on the body of the aborigine, it would have been impossible to conceive that a half century later he would be considered the greatest authority on the history and culture of the dead boy's tribe.

Because of the detailed preparations necessary before the expedition could take to the field, the party stayed at the fort for several weeks. The Army seemed eager to do everything it could to aid Marsh and his new science. General William Tecumseh Sherman gave him a letter of introduction that opened wide the door of every military post in the West, and, through his friendship with General Philip H. Sheridan, the paleontologist had received the promise of a military escort.[10] Major Frank North and two Pawnee scouts were given part of the job; about fifteen men of the 5th Cavalry would also go along.[11] North and his battalion of Pawnees were already famous in the West. In 1865 they had fought in the Powder River Campaign and, in 1869, in the Battle of Summit Springs. Perhaps their most important service for the encroaching white culture was in protecting the crews building the transcontinental railroad.

A day or two after Grinnell and his companions arrived at Fort McPherson, "Major Frank North, with two Pawnee Indians, appeared at the post, and we were taken out to the corral to choose our horses from a bunch of Indian ponies captured in the autumn of 1869 at the battle of Summit Springs, where Tall Bull's village of Cheyennes had been taken and Tall Bull and many of his people killed. There were some amusing scenes when these young men, many of whom had never mounted a horse, attempted to ride, but most of the horses were quite gentle and did not try to get rid of their riders."[12]

At last all preparations were complete, and the expedition, guided by the two Pawnee braves, struck out in the last days of July. "Except through what they had read, Professor Marsh and his party knew nothing about the West. It was an entirely innocent [body] ... of 'pilgrims,' starting out to face dangers of which they were wholly ignorant. ... The Sioux and Cheyenne ... occupied the country of western Nebraska and that to the north and northwest, and they objected strongly to the passage of people through their territory, and when they could do so — that is, when they believed they had the advantage — they attacked such parties. . . .

"We were blissfully ignorant of all this and supposed that because we saw no Indians, there were none about and that there was no danger. . . . Perhaps none of the eastern members of the party had ever before been very far out of sight of a house, and none could understand the possible danger of the situation, because all the surroundings were something entirely outside of their experience."[13]

It was not surprising then that "the members of the party ... were at first disposed to wander, not realizing that they might easily be lost, and quite as easily ... killed by Indians. Marsh was obliged to use strong language, and to summon to his aid Major North before he could keep the party together and with the escort."[14]

Curious to see how the "pilgrims" would handle themselves,

Cody accompanied the expedition on the first day's march. Around the campfire that night, Professor Marsh talked of the geological changes that had taken place in the land they were traveling through. Cody "was an interested auditor and was disposed to think that the professor was trying to see how much he could make his hearers believe of the stories he told them."[15]

Proceeding northward through the Sand Hills, they crossed the Dismal River, not far from where Grinnell, Cody and North would later run cattle, and then on to the middle fork of the Loup River. Here, Sioux graves were found. "They were on scaffolds, the bodies wrapped in robes and blankets. Arms [were] lying by their sides."[16]

Dead red men were not the only ones in evidence. "We found plenty of Indian sign . . . , and for about a week we were followed by Indians who were waiting for an opportunity to stampede the stock or get a little hair, but owing to the vigilance of Lieut. Reilly, our commanding officer, they were disappointed."[17] After many years of intimate association with aborigines, Grinnell would begin to manifest that profound empathy for them and their culture that make his writings so highly regarded. But, as yet, the wild Indian, like the wild animal, was simply a target. With a mixture of enthusiasm and disappointment, he wrote his parents: "Only one Indian was seen [in range] and no one was able to get a shot at him."[18]

But the Indians in camp — the two Pawnee scouts — were almost as interesting to Grinnell as those out on the prairie. "Both of them were celebrated, the oldest as a warrior and the youngest as a hunter. The oldest was named Tucky-tee-lous, which means, as . . . Major [North] explained it, 'the duellist,' or to give his own words: 'When he being alone meets a Sioux alone and they both shoot.' The younger [Pawnee] was named La-hoor-a-sac which means 'the best one of all.'

"When we first saw them they were clothed simply with moccasins, breech clouts and a blanket apiece, but before starting they were fitted out with a full suit of cavalry clothes, and although they were very proud and went around pointing to themselves and saying 'heap o' good,' it was easy to see that they were very uncomfortable. As soon as we got away from the fort, they took off everything but their shirts and pantaloons and packed them carefully away and did not take them out again until we got back.... Just before reaching the fort, they dressed up again [and] came in, in all their finery.

"They wore their hair long and had their scalp locks neatly braided, and sometimes they would decorate them with a piece of bright colored cloth or a feather. They were jolly fellows, both of them, and they would sing and dance for us frequently. There were not enough to have a war dance, but La-hoor-a-sac gave us the buffalo dance one night while Tucky-tee-lous sang.

"The last night in camp we had a good deal of fun. We all put on our blankets and marched in single file to the Indian tent, where we sat in a circle and smoked the pipe of peace. Then the major made a speech in Pawnee, La-hoor-a-sac answered him, and then Reeve, one of our fellows, made a stump speech to the Indians which, as they did not understand English, delighted them.... They sang the buffalo song,... we sang some college songs, and then the council broke up."[19]

Not all the nights in camp were as pleasant as this one. After stopping on the evening of July 21, the Marsh party found themselves confronted with an onrushing prairie fire that hostile aborigines may have set. "It was on the south bank of the [Loup] river and we were on the north bank. . . . At last, when the fire got just opposite us, it rushed down the bank into a clump of cedars and burnt furiously. We were afraid that it would cross and destroy everything. Lieut. Reilly ordered the bugle to sound the assembly, and the men fell in and were about to cross the river to try and put out the fire. At this moment the wind changed and soon after a heavy thunderstorm came up and partially extinguished the fire, so that there was no more danger from it."[20]

While there was the possibility of being killed by fire or Indians, a much more common danger resulted from the combination of a blazing sun and rationed water supply. During the five day march from the Platte north across the Sand Hills to the Loup, the men rode continuously in the open in temperatures as high as 110°, and the threat of sunstroke or heat exhaustion hung over every member of the expedition. "The hardest day's march ... was the second [one] ... out; we were 14 hours in the saddle without a drop of water except what we carried in our canteens. I never realized what thirst was before. Your mouth becomes perfectly dry and your lips split." With the romances of Mayne Reid ever in mind, Grinnell added: "The boys can [now] believe the descriptions of suffering . . . they read in Mayne Reid's books."[21]

Despite the lack of appeal the land held for humans, wild animals found it much to their liking. Big game was everywhere, including what some consider the grandest of Western trophies, the elk. "We saw two herds . . . and I went after both, but did not get one out of either herd. The first . . . contained from 200 to 250. We saw it about 9 A.M., the 19th [of July], and Lieut. Thomas sent a sergeant with one soldier . . . and myself to get some.[22] The elk were on the north bank [of the Loup] and we on the south. We went carefully along the river until we got a little beyond them. They did not pay any attention to us, but were gazing with curiosity at the command which was two or three miles down the river. We crossed and rode down on them through a belt of trees, but unfortunately just as we had got across, they smelt one of the Pawnees who was to windward of them, and away they went over the bluffs. We rode as hard as we could to the top of the bluffs to try to get a crack at them, but only arrived in time to see the last of the herd disappear over a bluff about half a mile away.

"The other herd came down the river one day when we were on [a ridge] . . . and although everybody fired at them, only one fawn was killed and that by a soldier. Several however were wounded, but we did not dare to follow them on account of Indians."[23]

By far the most abundant big game was the pronghorn antelope. "This was long prior to any settlement on the plains and the antelope were still nearly in their primitive numbers."[24] "Every day Major North took ahead with him one of the young men, whom he permitted to shoot at the antelope. No member of the party killed anything, which is not surprising in view of the fact that none of us knew anything of hunting or rifle shooting. . . ."[25] As a result, it was "Major North and the Indians [who] kept us supplied with fresh meat."[26]

Following the Loup westward, the expedition investigated Miocene and Pliocene fossil deposits. As usual, while the geologists dug in the low areas, the soldiers stood guard on the bluffs above. After turning south, the party struck the North Platte, and then traveled east, back to Fort McPherson.[27] From there, they boarded a train for Fort D. A. Russell near Cheyenne, Wyoming. "Here I had my first experience with a bucking horse and was twice ingloriously thrown. J. M. Russell then mounted the horse, which went off quietly."[28] Using the fort as a base, a trip was made south to some buttes containing Miocene beds, then east for an undetermined distance, north to the North Platte at Scottsbluff, Nebraska, for more Miocene deposits, and finally, west, back to Fort Russell.[29]

It was on this second trip that Grinnell and a friend lost their "pilgrim" status. On the morning of August 20 while camped on Horse Creek, a small stream that flows into the North Platte, Professor Marsh asked Grinnell and Jack Nicholson to bag some ducks for the evening meal.[30] A cavalry officer, who supposedly knew the country, stated that the course of the creek ran southwest in a relatively straight line. Since the wagon train was moving in the same direction and presumably parallel to the creek, "we were told not to pay any attention to the movements of the column but to follow the creek until we came to the night's camp."[31] What no one knew was that between the morning and night camps, a distance of about twenty miles, the creek made a great bend of approximately sixty-five miles.

Grinnell and his companion set out at 6:30 A.M. It was not long before they noticed that the column was going out of sight, but "we supposed that this was only to find a road for the wagons."[32] After following the creek for fifteen miles, enough ducks were shot for the evening meal. Now noon, they had not sighted the party again since it first disappeared, and the two men were in the middle of country inhabited by hostile Cheyenne and Sioux. Having become increasingly anxious, they decided to leave the creek to try and find the trail. They "rode up on to some high hills to see if the camp was in sight" but saw nothing except an endless sweep of rolling prairie.[33] By this time, their anxiety was approaching panic.

At the point where they left the creek was another grave like those found earlier. This man, however, had died much more recently. "His knife, which was by him, was not rusted, and his long black hair looked fresh."[34] Even in his fear, Grinnell stopped to marvel at "the fact that a pair of barn swallows had commenced a nest on the underpart of the litter he was laid on."[35] How curious, he thought, that a mighty Dakota warrior, perhaps with many scalps, should now have his own hairs removed to line the nest of tiny birds.

"After examining the Sioux, but without disturbing him, we struck off southwest to look for the trail. We travelled along for 7 or 8 miles, and suddenly to our great astonishment struck the creek again. For a few moments we thought we must have come in a circle but on looking at our land marks, we saw that we had kept a straight course, and that the river bent around almost at right angles with its former course. We then determined to follow the creek as we were sure of water while on it.

"About this time, 2 or 3 P.M., we saw a smoke in the east. At first we were afraid it was an Indian signal fire, . . . but after watching it awhile we saw that it was the prairie burning. We hurried along the creek, and when the flames got within about half a mile of us, I got off my horse and fired the creek bottom; after doing this, as the flames seemed to advance slowly, we mounted and rode on, but after going a few hundred yards I thought it safer to get off and set the grass ahead on fire again. The fire seemed about [a] quarter of a mile off when I dismounted and . . . gave my horse to Jack to hold, and also my gun. I had set the fire going in two places and was lighting a match for the third, when suddenly I heard Jack scream to me 'mount Birdie mount.' I knew by his tone that there was danger, so without looking round I jumped on my horse and then turned to take my gun from him. At that moment the fire was not twenty feet from us, the flames were 5 or 6 feet high, and the air was so hot and filled with smoke that we could not breathe. As soon as I was on my horse we both put spurs to the animals and galloped down in to the bottom where it was burnt. Jack said that he sat with his eyes on the fire the whole time, and that it moved very slowly until it got within about 200 yards of us, and that then it took the immense leap which almost reached us."[36] While they escaped real harm, the fire did come "near enough to singe the hair on our faces and on the horses."[37]

"After the fire had passed, we travelled along the creek till nearly sunset. We then gave up all hope of finding the camp that night, and going down into a small gulch where there was grass we unsaddled and made as if we were going to camp there. We watered our horses and picketed them where they could get the best food, and then Jack and I cleaned and ate a saw duck.[38] We had no wood, and if we . . . had, we would not have dared to build a fire for fear of Indians. After our duck Jack and I had a talk over our chances, and we decided that they were very small. We thought that in all probability, the Indians had been watching us all day from the bluffs, and that at night they would come down and lift our hair, or . . . would lay for us next day and as we were crossing some canon, . . . shoot us before we saw them. Another thing that made us uneasy was the fact that we were without rifles. [They had only shotguns.] The noble red men might come up within a hundred yards, and stand there and fire shot after shot till we were both killed. We determined that our best plan was to follow our own trail back to camp, and there to strike the wagon trail and follow it up."[39] No matter how long it took, this was the only sure way of finding the command.

"By this time, it was pitch dark and we thought we would try and [play] . . . a little game on the Red Man. We therefore saddled up and moved quietly down the bed of the stream for a few hundred yards and then leaving the water, we pushed on for about a mile and a half. Then after looking for a place, we went into camp for the night. By good luck I had my poncho strapped to my saddle, and that with the saddle blankets formed our bed. We did not dare to trust our horses to the picket pins, for the ground was very soft, and we were afraid that they might get away; so we tied the lariats round our legs, and attempted to sleep. We did not get much rest however, for every time a bird or an animal rustled in the bushes, we would sit up and listen; and then too Jack's horse had a trick of pulling up his picket pin by jerking on his lariat, and when the rope was around J's leg, you may suppose at each jerk Jack would go flying through the air."[40] One time during the night, he was "dragged twelve or fifteen feet out into the prairie, while I, under the impression that this was the beginning of an Indian attack, sat up with my shotgun across my knees, determined to sell my life as dearly as possible."[41]

"As the first grey broke in the east, we saddled up and started down the creek; we saw I suppose 500 antelope, but as we had no rifles could not get any. On reaching the Sioux grave we stopped, and while I built a small fire, Jack cleaned a couple of ducks, and we made a hearty breakfast. It is true that the entrails had turned green, and that they smelt stronger than anything I ever saw before, but nevertheless, I think that I never ate anything that tasted so good."[42] What a strange sight that must have been as two frightened men greedily tore at their food under the shadow of the dead Sioux!

"We were now getting rather tired, and the constant anxiety was so great that Jack was almost done up, and I myself was feeling pretty badly discouraged. After our breakfast I wanted to hurry right on, while Jack had given up in despair. He wanted to stay where he was and wouldn't come on. After working at him for awhile, I got him up and we started. About 3 miles from the old camp, I struck across south, and about 3 miles from the water I struck the trail. I was about 30 yards ahead looking for it, and Jack's horse was following mine, his rider . . . doubled up on the saddle, paying no attention to anything. You can't imagine the sense of relief and joy . . . felt when I saw the trail. I gave a whoop, and Jack roused by the noise rode up and we shook hands delightedly. We followed the trail and reached camp late in the afternoon. Of course we were received with congratulations, for no one in camp ever expected to see us again. Early the day we got in, some of the soldiers picked up an Indian pony, and it was supposed by everyone in the outfit that we were killed, and that the Indians after taking our horses and traps, had turned this pony loose because he was lame."[43]

The experience had been a terrifying one but in retrospect, Grinnell, at least, was exuberant: "I am happy to say that though there were scouting parties out after us all day, we made our way into camp without any assistance from anyone."[44] Confronted with a variety of the worst perils the Western wilderness had to offer, he had survived, earning the right to shed the pilgrim status. Mayne Reid would have approved.

Returning to Fort Russell, the expedition boarded a train for Fort Bridger, founded in 1843 by the most famous of the mountain men. On the Oregon Trail, it was located in what is now southwest Wyoming. "This was then the home of Judge Carter, of the great contracting firm of Coe and Carter, which for years had been famous in the western country.[45] Judge Carter, then perhaps fifty years old, with his wife and young daughters, kept open house at the old fort with true southern hospitality. Dr. Carter, said to be related to the family and a very nice young fellow, had charge of the trading store which still supplied goods to the Indians of the region, as it had from the old days when Fort Bridger was first established.[46]

"The post was on the way between the country of the Snake or Shoshoni Indians, about Fort Washaki[e] to the north, and the agency of the Uinta Utes at Fort Uinta. The trail between Fort Bridger and Fort Uinta, then the only permanent camp in the country of the Uinta Utes, crossed Henry's Fork of Green River.

"Down on the White River, to the east of Fort Uinta, at an earlier day, had stood an old trading post said to have been established by the old St. Louis fur trader, Robidoux.

"Fort Bridger was not an active place, but its situation was delightful. A few soldiers were stationed there, and it was still a military post. From time to time, groups of Indians from south or north camped near it, stayed for a little while, sold their furs or purchased goods at the trader's store, and then went on. To people who had just come in from two or three months spent on the hot dry plains to the eastward, the post with its timber, its green grass, and its trout streams, seemed very attractive.

"About the fort were two or three old-time dwellers in the West, of whom one of the most interesting was Uncle Jack Robinson. It was said that he had come into the country as early as 1834, and he spoke of events that had happened more than thirty years before. Uncle Jack said that he was one of the party of trappers that found in an abandoned Indian camp an Arapaho child who for some cause had been left behind by his people. He was named Friday, because that was the day of the week on which he was found. . . . The trappers took this child with them, cared for him, and later sent him on to St. Louis, where it was said that he had been educated, trained in theology, and finally, sent out to become a missionary 'to snatch his people from the burning.'

"It was from Uncle Jack Robinson that I first heard the tale of the extinguishment of the buffalo on the Laramie plains in 1840 or about then. It was the familiar story of a very deep snow followed by a thaw, and that by severe cold which froze a crust so hard that the buffalo could not get through it, and so starved to death. In 1870 their skeletons were still to be seen in many places on the Laramie plains, and the cause assigned for their extermination . . . was no doubt the true one.

"Uncle Jack . . . was a kindly, friendly man and very ready to talk with the youngsters who questioned him. It is a great pity that some of them did not know enough to ask the old man for a multitude of details about his experiences, and to set them down."[47]

After examining fossil deposits near Fort Bridger, the Marsh party planned to journey south, crossing Henry's Fork of the Green River, travel down the latter to the junction of the White River, go up the White an indefinite distance, and then head north for the return trip over the mountains to the fort.[48] But before setting out through this rough terrain, Grinnell wanted to obtain a reliable mount: "The little horse that I was riding was a partly broken colt, that did not yet know the rope, frequently broke loose and ran off, and caused me many unnecessary steps. . . . But I could hear of no one that had horses for sale until finally it was suggested that I might procure one at a camp over on Henry's Fork of Green River, where some trappers were camped who had . . . horses. Accordingly, one morning I set out to visit this camp.

"I recall pleasantly . . . the ride through the cool, fresh day from Fort Bridger to Henry's Fork. The mountains and their animals were new to me. I was young and enthusiastic and enjoyed all that I saw. Some time before reaching Henry's Fork, the trail approached a narrow stream, only four or five feet wide, cut into the soil through a flat sage brush prairie and without any timber near it. As I neared this stream, not far from the trail, I saw a wake in the water caused by some creature swimming down the stream and just beneath the surface. I jumped off my horse, twisted his rope about a sage brush and ran lightly forward to the edge of the brook and, a moment later, saw swimming toward me beneath the surface, a small beaver, the first I had ever seen. When it was opposite . . . and just below me, I fired . . . and the little thing turned over and came to the surface . . . to be captured.

"It was almost sundown when I reached Henry's Fork, and following a well-worn trail, approached a little camp of three buffalo skin lodges standing close together along the stream. As I rode into the camp, Ike Edwards came in from another direction, and we met and I explained my errand. He took me into his lodge, and gave me food, and a little later I met the other men. John Baker and Phil Mass each had a Shoshoni wife and . . . a large flock of children of various sizes. . . . Ike Edwards told me to turn my horse out into the general horse herd which was feeding nearby, and gave me robes and blankets for my bed; then by the small lodge fire, which was needed for light only and not for warmth, we talked far into the night. The following morning we were all early astir and before breakfast two men had gone up the stream and two down, to look at their traps. Ike Edwards and I found two beaver in two of his traps but the others had not been disturbed. The traps were reset with the usual care, the heavy beaver tied on the horses, and we returned to camp to breakfast.

"I spent some time that morning watching the men skin their beaver, for those who had gone up the stream had also captured two. It was the first time I had ever seen beaver skinned, and the fact that a stroke of a knife had to be made for every bit of skin that was lifted from the body was a revelation to me. Somewhat later I rode out to the horse herd and made a bargain with Phil Mass by which my little colt [was] . . . traded for an older, broken, hunting horse.

"The life in this camp was an ideal one. All about in the stream bottom, on the hills, and among the mountains, there was game — birds, deer, antelope, and at a distance, elk. The stream furnished trout in uncounted numbers, and a certain amount of fur. The men had each a few cows which ranged about in the river bottom and were driven in morning and evening to be milked. It was really a place where every prospect seemed to please. The habitations of the men were, as already said, tanned buffalo skin lodges, and the camp was rather a permanent one so that the bed . . . and fireplaces were built up to be comfortable and useful. There was plenty of food, plenty of covering, and plenty of shelter. In such a situation no one could suffer.

"Edwards was a very tall man with a thin, shrewd, but handsome . . . face, kindly, friendly, humorous, and as I learned from

other people at a later day, a man of great daring, an excellent
hunter, and a most skillful trapper. As we rode back toward the
lodges that morning, I watched him with great interest, and two
or three times when the half-broken horse that he was riding shied
or sprang to one side, it was interesting to see those long legs wrap
themselves about the little animal's body. Edwards had come from
New England, and as we talked about the East and the old times,
he made some jesting allusions to his ancestor, Jonathan Edwards.

"John Baker had come out into the western country sometime
between 1838 and 1840 in company with his more famous brother,
Jim. He had lost a leg, but this in no degree interfered with his
riding, and he had long lived a trapper's life, probably not profit-
ing greatly, but he had now all that heart could wish for, and only
the settling up of the country could interfere with his continued
peace and prosperity.

"Phil Mass was a Mexican who had come up from the south,
a splendid man physically, tall, broad, massive, and of great
strength, yet light and active on his feet. He was more quiet and
reserved than any of the others, with the polish and suavity of a
real hidalgo.

"All these men were dressed in the costume that prevailed in
the early days of plains travel and persisted until 1875 or later.
Coats, shirts, trousers, and moccasins were of soft tanned buckskin, fringed along the seams, ornamented with stained porcupine
quills or with beads, and the coats in some cases trimmed at cuffs
and about the collar with beaver fur. The fringe on the seams was
in part for ornament, but also had its practical value, for it furnished strings for tying, lacing, and mending different articles
that had been damaged.

"These men lived in just the fashion of the old-time trappers of
early western days. They possessed that independence which all
men seek. Theirs was everything that man needs — food, clothing,
shelter, and family. They were masters of their own lives. When
they felt like it, they pulled down their lodges, packed their pos-
sessions on their animals, and moved away to another place which
pleased them, and their home was there so long as they wished.
In winter, they camped in sheltered places or moved into comfortable log houses. The pursuit of food, the attention to their
traps, and the care of their livestock lent to their lives an interest

which never failed. Their mode of life appealed strongly to a young man fond of the open, and while I was with them I could not imagine, nor can I imagine now, a more attractive — a happier — life than theirs. Yet at any time its attractions might be altered or ended by an influx of population that would crowd these men out of their happy surroundings. As a matter of fact, such an influx did come, but not until many years after the time of which I write.

"The time spent in this old-time camp was full of joy and interest. In the morning we visited the traps, and later in the day I rode with Edwards or Baker up and down the stream or off into the hills. I saw Edwards make a remarkable shot at a running deer; and one morning his quick eye detected a wildcat on a branch in a cottonwood tree, which he pointed out to me and which I shot."[49] In a sense, these were the men the romantic young Easterner had come West to find. "I desired enormously to spend the rest of my life with these people, but, of course, the knowledge of the grief this would give my parents pulled me back again."[50]

With keen regret, Grinnell left the trappers' camp. Although he would see them only once more, as the Marsh expedition passed south on its way to White River, he learned years later that the foreman of his Wyoming ranch married a woman who was the same baby Grinnell had seen in the lodge of John Baker a generation before.[51]

"From Fort Bridger and Henry's Fork we went south along Green River to Brown's Hole, then down to White River, up to the Uinta Ute Reservation, above old Fort Robidoux, and thence back to Bridger."[52] "There were no roads and travel with wagons was impossible. With some difficulty the journey was made by pack trains."[53] Grinnell has left a graphic account of the Green River country: "From where it rises — a little brook in Fremont's Peak — the Green River rolls southward an impetuous torrent, its volume constantly increasing as it receives the tribute brought by a thousand channels from the lofty mountains through which it flows. Its waters are dark and black as it sweeps through some narrow passage where the sun's rays never penetrate, but assume when spread out in the clear light of day the pale green color from which it takes its name.

"It is a glorious river. The territory through which it passes presents some of the most majestic scenery that our country can afford. For miles it rushes through deep and gloomy cañons, whose precipitous sides offer no inequality that might serve as the resting place for a bird; or through stony valleys, where the water leaps and dashes against the rocks as though they were enemies, that it would tear from their beds and carry captive toward the Colorado. It roars between high mountains, rock-ribbed and dark with their evergreen foliage, or sublime with their mantles of everlasting snows, and glides pleasantly through fertile valleys, where Nature is the only husbandman and . . . deer and elk the only cattle. . . .

"In time, the sportsman or naturalist will find here much to attract and delight him. And perhaps he may even be tempted, as I once was, to sever for a time the ties that bind him to his eastern home, and, building a little cabin, settle in this country until he shall have exhausted its pleasures. . . .

"Fifty miles below the Union Pacific Railroad crossing, the river becomes wider, and its mad rush for awhile is checked as it flows slowly through a broad valley. Here its surface is dotted with little sand bars, against which the water ripples with a gentle murmur, far different from its usual angry roar. On the north and south the mountains, stern and immutable in their rugged magnificence, form an almost continuous barrier, and seem to open unwillingly the narrow channel through which the waters pass. On the east the bluffs rise one after another in bare, gray walls until they become part of the foothills and at last run into the mountains a few miles away. On the west the valley is bounded by a range of lofty buttes, almost perpendicular on every side, but occasionally affording a path by which an active climber may reach the summit. . . .

"Near the base of one of these buttes our camp is pitched. Three or four tents, their white canvas showing bright against the green willows, stand at a short distance from the water. Four Government wagons are drawn up not far off, and the baggage of the outfit lies on the ground beside them. The horses and mules, dispersed over the plain, are cropping the luxuriant herbage, tended by their watchful herders, who occasionally drive in those that stray too far, and prevent the more restless from wandering away from camp.

"Around the glowing fire a dozen men are stretched upon the

ground. Bearded, bronzed by exposure to all weathers, and clothed in buckskin, you might take them all at first glance for a party of trappers; but their speech betrays their occupation, and shows you that they are members of some scientific expedition.

"The evening meal over, they have lighted their pipes, and are discussing with animated voice and gesture the various prizes obtained during the day. Some exult in a new fossil; others examine some rare bird; others still are looking over their tools, while two, who are cleaning their rifles, converse about to-morrow's hunt. The two last are John N. [icholson] and myself. The last morsel of fresh meat in the camp has been consumed to-day, and we have resolved to make an early start to-morrow morning and see if we cannot renew the supply. So, soon after the sun goes down we wrap our buffalo robes around us and ere long are soundly asleep.

"The stars were shining brightly from the cloudless sky, when we crossed the river and turning north, directed our course up the stream. The wind blew chilly down from the mountains, causing us to gather our blankets closer about us [as] we trotted silently along. At length we reached a deep and rocky cañon, where, on passing some days before, we had noticed numerous tracks of deer and elk; here, turning away from the river, we commenced to ascend the heights.

"A silent ride of about two miles between the gloomy rocks brought us to the commencement of the timber just as the light began to appear in the East. Pushing on through this until we were well up on the mountain, we came to a slight opening among the pines, where a little spring bubbling out of the ground fertilized a small extent of land and nourished a rich growth of grass. Here we halted and unsaddled our horses, and after picketing them out to feed, started off to look for . . . game. . . .

"We took the precaution to notice with the utmost care the various landmarks that we passed on our way. This was necessary for the reason that among those extensive forests, each tree looks so much like the next one that unless great care is exercised, the traveler, becoming bewildered by this similarity, is almost sure to lose his way.

"As we proceed through the sombre aisles of the forest, our

moccasin-shod feet fall noiselessly upon the thick carpet of fine needles with which the ground is spread. The breeze blows softly on our faces, bringing with it the faint damp odors of decaying vegetation, and soughs with a gentle rustling through the tops of the lofty pines. A dim, uncertain light pervades the scene, rarely relieved by a ray of sunlight, which breaks through the dense foliage and flecks the ground with spangles of waving gold. The ruffed grouse, with sedate step and dignified bearing, stalks a few paces away from our path, while the little pine squirrel, startled from the ground, hurries to some elevated perch, whence he gazes at us with his round, black eyes, wondering, no doubt, what the strange creatures are that invade these mysterious solitudes. No sound is heard save the whispering of the pines and the distant cry of the Clarke's crow, borne faintly to our ears from the peaks above.

"At length we reach a spot where the trees grow farther apart and the light becomes stronger, and as we round the prostrate trunk of a huge tree, an object catches our eye which causes us suddenly to stand motionless as statues. A fine . . . buck is feeding on the edge of the opening not seventy-five yards from us. The wind blowing from him to us has not notified him of our presence, nor have his eyes or ears warned him to hurry away through the forest. We draw cautiously back to the shelter of the fallen tree, John kneels, and as the buck presents his side, fires. The crack of the rifle echoes over the mountain and is thrown back from a hundred crags. The buck gives two or three sudden bounds and stands gazing wildly around for a moment, and then moves slowly off through the trees. But we have seen the life blood pouring from the wound behind his shoulder, and we know that he will not go far before lying down. . . .

"We step leisurely forward to the spot where he disappeared and find a thick trail of blood, and following this for about thirty yards we come to the beautiful creature lying dead, his muscles still quivering. . . ."[54]

After skinning and breaking up the quarry, the two men continue their hunt. Both have had enough rifle practice the last few weeks to make them fair shots. As a result, they are able to bag three more deer by late afternoon.

"Hastily bleeding the game, we hurry off to bring up the horses. And we were none too soon in doing so. The time taken in packing the loads, and in looking for John's [second] buck, . . . and the fact that we had to walk, leading our burdened horses, delayed us so that the sun was setting as we emerged from the timber. A little later and we should have been forced to camp in the forest. No great hardship, . . . true, but we preferred the dinner that awaited us in camp and our warm buffalo robes to dry deer meat and a single blanket in the mountains.

"We hurried down the cañon, and in a short time after reaching the river bank were opposite the camp. Here our shouts soon attracted the attention of the crowd around the fire, and a couple of horses were led over to us by one of the party, which we mounted and rode across the river. And now while we enjoy our dinner by the cheerful fire-light, some skin the last three deer and others tell us of what they have done during the day and demand an account of our trip. This is soon given; and when an hour later the rising moon silvers the mountains, the plain and the river, and floods the camp with its clear, pale light, . . . no sound breaks the stillness of the air save the monotonous cropping of the feeding herd and the low murmur of the water as it ripples softly against the banks. . . ."[55]

The journey of Grinnell and his companions back over the Uinta Mountains to Fort Bridger was another great adventure. Crossing the range by way of a pass 11,000 feet high, the pack train wound a circuitous course through the rugged country, halting only temporarily at potential fossil fields.

The members of the expedition did not spend all their time in traveling and collecting, however, as is shown by Grinnell's account of a grouse hunt: It is early morning and "we are camped by a pleasant stream among the Uintah [sic] mountains in Wyoming.[56] North, south, east and west the eye rests upon mountains piled on mountains. Some covered to their summits with dark green conifers, others ragged and rough with immense masses of rock, and [cut] . . . with deep cañons, between the precipitous sides of which hurry in spring the melted snows which gather to swell the volume of the mighty Colorado as it sweeps toward the Pacific. Still on every side, but farther away, lofty and now glistening, as one by one they are touched by the growing light, rise others, crowned with eternal snows. . . .

"Four of us, . . . tired of continual 'bone digging,' had determined to devote a short time to pleasure alone, and our chief, Prof. M. [arsh], assenting, [we] had started off to have a day with the sage grouse.

"Jack N. [icholson], Johnny G. [riswold] and Jim R. [ussell], three royal fellows with myself made up the quartette, and we had taken Joe along to cook and keep camp. . . .[57]

"We had left the main camp on the afternoon of the previous day, and travelling fifteen miles before evening, had reached a point about ten miles from our shooting ground. Our outfit was of the lightest, as we expected to be away only for a day or two. Rifles had been laid aside for the time, and we carried only our double-barrels with a sufficiency of No. 6 shot and C. & H. powder. Tents had been left behind as an unnecessary luxury, and a single pack mule . . . , on account of the roughness of the trail, sufficed to carry all our effects.

"A shout from Joe summoned the remaining sleepers, and a few minutes were devoted to a hasty toilet. Then comes breakfast, consisting of trout caught from the stream the evening before, and ducks shot on the march. That over and the pipes lighted, we collect our horses, which have been grazing over the creek bottom, and saddling them and packing our mule we are soon under way. . . .

"Our destination was a little park in the mountains on the banks of the same creek on which we had camped. At this point the bottom was wider than usual, and the bluffs which bordered it, instead of forming merely the lowest benches of the foot hills, stretched out in a plain several miles in extent. On all sides, except where the stream entered and passed out, the mountains rose in a stately wall, forbidding and impassable. This plain, intersected by one or two small brooks and covered with sage brush, was where we expected to find the grouse. . . .

"We rode silently along until we reached the park, where we made camp and prepared for action. Dividing our forces, we started off in opposite directions. Each pair was to follow the plain along its edge, skirting the base of the mountains until they reached one of the little brooks that entered it at various points. This they were to follow down, beating on both sides until they came to the main stream. Jack and Jimmy went south and John and myself north."[58]

After a two mile walk, Grinnell and his companion came "to the foothills and . . . the locality where we might expect to find birds. The numerous ravines which run down from the mountains, bringing the waters of winter and spring from the high ground, were still moist and . . . filled with a luxuriant growth of vegetation. Here were occasional pools frequented [by] . . . ducks, and on the margins of which we noticed the tracks of deer, elk and bear.

"The first of these pools which we approached was covered with mallards and black ducks. . . ."[59] Carefully drawing near, we had advanced within easy gunshot before being perceived by the birds, and as they sprang up were enabled to give our four barrels, dropping two in the water and two more in the high grass. To have lain in wait here for the ducks that were continually flying would have been grand sport, but eager to get at the grouse, we merely stopped to pick up our birds and then pushed on. As we walked along, the faint echoes of distant shots saluted our ears and notified us that our comrades on the other side of the valley were already at work.

"We reached the brook, and John, pushing aside the willows which at this point lined its banks, was stepping across it, when almost from under his feet sprang a pack of ruffed grouse . . . which with much bustle flew off toward the mountains. Not swiftly enough, however, to escape his ready gun, for snapping at them as soon as his feet touched the opposite bank, the last bird turned neatly over to the shot, while his companions with hurried flappings disappeared up the ravine.

"Before proceeding far down the stream we came upon the first flock of sage grouse. There were only about a dozen of them, but beckoning John over, we went toward them. They paid little attention to us until we were within forty yards. . . . As soon, however, as they lost the hope of escaping unobserved, they got up with a good deal of noise, uttering a clucking cry not unlike that of a hen when frightened.

"The old cock that flew first fell to John's right barrel, and the next two I stopped before they had got far, while John, who shot beautifully all that day, made a long shot at a fourth, killing it clean. . . . The flock had scattered badly, and as we knew the futility of trying to find the birds when once frightened, we kept on down the stream looking for a fresh lot.

"Two more flocks had been found from which we had secured five birds, when noticing that it was long past noon, lunch was suggested. It was a scanty meal, consisting of the remains of our breakfast, but it was heartily enjoyed and at its close a pleasant lazy half hour was spent in the enjoyment of a cigarette. At length we rose to our feet about to resume our guns, when a splash was heard in the brook below, which we knew must have been made by a beaver. Stepping quietly down to the water's edge we were looking about for it, when suddenly I saw John throw forward his gun and fire into the water, and then stooping down draw forth a little beaver kitten about eighteen inches long. John had fired at it as he saw it swimming under the water without exactly knowing what it was he shot. With a sigh for his untimely fate, the little fellow was added to our bag and we hurried forward.

"The birds seemed to become more numerous as we approached the main stream. We no longer crossed over when a flock was discovered, but each shot what he could of those on his own side. At last when we reached the creek and sat down to rest and count our birds, we found John's bag to consist of seventeen sage grouse, two ducks, one ruffed grouse, and the little beaver. I had not done quite so well, having only sixteen sage grouse, two ducks and a snow goose . . . , that scared by John had flown from the brook and crossed before me within easy gun shot. The thirty-nine birds made a pretty heavy bag, and with what we expected our companions to bring in would be enough to supply the main camp with birds for some days.

"As we were gathering up our game we heard a faint shout, and turning saw Jack and Jim hastening toward us. They were fairly loaded down with birds, and in answer to our inquiries, produced twelve mallards and black ducks, twenty-one sage grouse, three ruffed grouse, and five blue-winged teal. . . . The teal had all fallen at a single shot which Jimmy had fired into the flock as they rose from the water. The numbers of ducks that our friends had seen at the head of the stream had caused them to linger there so long that they had finally been forced by the approach of night to hurry toward camp, rather neglecting the grouse, although from their account these must have been as plentiful on their ground as on ours.

"We were soon in camp, where we found Joe, who had not passed the day in idleness. A dozen or more silvery trout lay upon the grass, and near them the saddle and hams of a yearling buck, which Joe had killed while on his fishing excursion down the creek. He had prepared everything for supper, and ere long the savory odors that rose from our camp fire would have attracted men less hungry than we. . . .

"Fish, flesh and fowl . . . combined to allay the 'rage of hunger,' and we sat around the fire talking of the day and its incidents, of by-gone years and future plans. . . . But at length the camp grew . . . quiet, the fire burned down, and knocking the ashes from our pipes, we wrapped our blankets around us and one by one lay down to dream of our day with the sage grouse."[60]

Grinnell and his companions rejoined Marsh the next afternoon, and a few days later the party reached Fort Bridger. Shortly after returning to the post, Grinnell had the "interesting experience of driving stage for the distance of eleven miles, from the Fort to Bridger Station on the U.P.R.R. [Union Pacific Railroad], and back. The driver, whom I remember as Charley, and whom I had accompanied on one or two trips, got hurt and I took his place for a few days. The mules we drove were pack animals, unbroken to harness. They had to be roped, tied up, harnessed, and . . . by force hitched to the stage. . . ." Then "the way [was] cleared and the mules . . . let go. For the first six or seven miles of the road, the frightened animals ran as hard as they could, and the drive was . . . exciting, but coming back from the railroad station they went quietly enough."[61]

Leaving Fort Bridger, the Marsh party went to Salt Lake City where the Professor and Grinnell called on Brigham Young.[62] The group then continued on to California, which was reached in early November. Here, a trip was made to Yosemite Valley and the Mariposa Grove of Big Trees (giant sequoias). From San Francisco most of the expedition, including Grinnell, returned to the

Grinnell in 1870,
the year he first went west.

"The Hemlocks," Grinnell's home in Audubon Park.

Lucy Bakewell Audubon.

Audubon Park. The lithograph shows the naturalist's home
and the Hudson near what is now 156th Street.

Grinnell's "bird room"

Camp on the 1870 Marsh expedition. The man second from the left is probably Grinnell.

Cheyenne, Wyoming, on the eve of the Marsh expedition's visit.

The 1870 Marsh expedition in Chicago on its way to the Great West. Standing, left to right, are John Reed Nicholson, Grinnell, James W. Wadsworth, Marsh, Charles Wyllys Betts, Harry Degen Ziegler, Henry Bradford Sargent; sitting are John Wool Griswold, Alexander Hamilton Ewing, Eli Whitney, Charles McCormick Reeve, and James Russell.

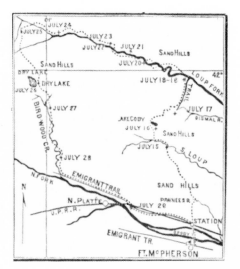

First side trip of
the 1870 Marsh expedition.

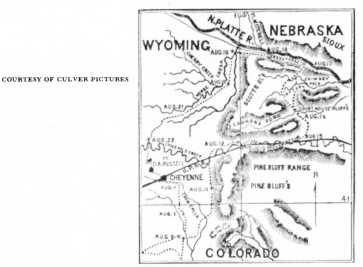

Second side trip of
1870 Marsh expedition.

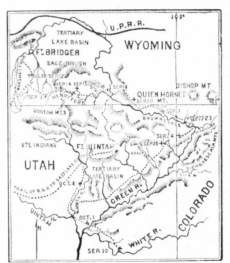

Third side trip of
.1870 Marsh expedition.

The 1870 Marsh expedition in the field near Fort Bridger. Marsh is standing in the center, directly behind the stovepipe, and the man standing second to his right, in the wide-brimmed hat, is Grinnell.

Omaha about 1870, when the town was on the edge of the frontier.

Painting showing the use of live steam to frighten buffalo away from the tracks.

The hide hunter's work: forty thousand buffalo hides at Dodge City, Kansas, 1876.

Even after the hide hunters had exterminated the buffalo, there was one more harvest to be gathered from that hapless animal. Countless tons of rotting bones were hauled to the railroads and shipped east to be ground into fertilizer.

Fort Bridger, one of the posts visited by the 1870 Marsh expedition.

Laramie, Wyoming Territory, shortly before the 1870 Marsh expedition passed through the settlement. Note the three freshly killed antelope (counting the one on the ground behind the men).

"Permanent" Pawnee village of earth lodges, Genoa, Nebraska, circa 1872.

Ute camp in Middle Park, Colorado, in the 1870's.

Ute Indians in Middle Park, Colorado, in the 1870's.

Scaffold burials of the plains Indian, like the ones found on the 1870 Marsh expedition. These are of Crow Indians in Montana.

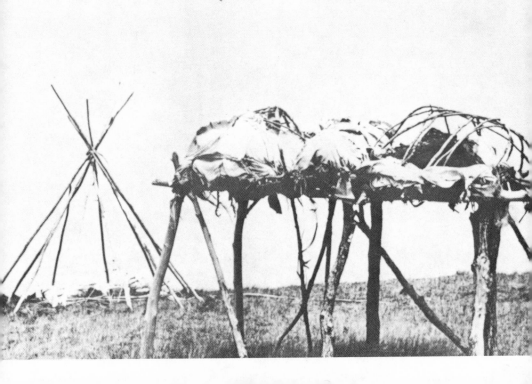

Temple Street, Salt Lake City, Utah, circa 1869.

Hot Sulphur Springs, Middle Park, Colorado, in the 1870's.

Fort Berthold, Dakota Territory.

Camp (Fort) Baker, Montana Territory.

Fort Buford, Dakota Territory.

The Colorado River flowing through Middle Park, Colorado; 1874.

Frank North.

Luther North.

William H. Reed in 1879.

East; he reached New York City about Thanksgiving. A few of the assistants stayed with Marsh and went to Kansas. There they collected Cretaceous fossils until the bitter cold of December drove them home.[63]

After five months in the unmapped West, the Marsh expedition was back. Not merely the scientific community but the American public at large was eager to learn the results of the exploration. Over one hundred species of extinct vertebrates new to science were brought back, including toothed birds, fossil horses, and a pterodactyl.[64] These fossils provided the best documentation to date of the validity of evolutionary theory. Stored in Yale's Peabody Museum, they were the foundation of Marsh's later work, among which was *Odontornithes — A Monograph on the Extinct Toothed Birds of North America* (1880). When the book appeared, Charles Darwin himself wrote Marsh stating that in the twenty year period since the *Origin of Species* was published, no one had done as much to confirm its basic conclusions.[65]

The 1870 expedition was important for another reason — it was the harbinger of a new era in Western exploration. According to William Goetzmann, "the country beyond the Mississippi, as we now know it, was not just 'discovered' in one dramatic and colorful era of early-nineteenth-century coonskin exploration. Rather, it was discovered and rediscovered by generations of very different explorers down through the centuries."[66] Marsh's odyssey marked the start of a new cycle of rediscovery set in motion by a rising generation concerned with more sophisticated problems than their predecessors. Once, the explorer was content to find a mountain; now, he wanted to know how the mountain came into being, and what life existed on its slopes in the dim past. Grinnell was in the vanguard of the ascending generation of more sophisticated explorers, and his awareness of the great transformations the earth had undergone made him recognize that the land was not invulnerable as most of his contemporaries seemed to believe. His study of fossil animals taught him that the long-term survival of a species was the exception, not the rule. When the concept of a vulnerable natural world was taken out of the past and applied to his own time, it naturally led to a new concern for the land. As this concern spread, a new cycle of rediscovery would begin —

the West would then be conceived as a field for developing and testing the concepts of conservation. This was the culmination of the more sophisticated orientation toward the West begun by Marsh's 1870 expedition.

3

Hunting
Buffalo and Elk

WHEN GRINNELL RETURNED to New York, he found his father determined to plan his future. "It had been my hope to study medicine," Grinnell recalled in his MEMOIRS, "but on talking it over with my father I found that he was anxious to have me go into business, to relieve him, and ultimately to take his place. This seemed the proper thing to do," and "I entered my father's office at 36 Broad Street, as a clerk without pay."[1]

"At that time my father was the principal agent in Wall Street of Commodore Cornelius Vanderbilt, who controlled the New York Central system of railroads. Horace F. Clark, Commodore Vanderbilt's son-in-law, and a man of great ability, was special partner in the firm. Somewhat later, Mr. Clark, Augustus Schell, and James H. Bancker, acquired control of the Lake Shore and Michigan Southern Railroad Company, the Chicago and North-western Railroad Co., and the Union Pacific R.R."[2]

Although "the business of Geo. B. Grinnell & Co. was large and profitable," the younger Grinnell had little interest in it. Instead, "my long trip in the West had resulted in a close acquaintance

with Marsh and a deep interest in scientific matters."[3] The paleontologist encouraged Grinnell, showing him that his fascination
with birds could lead to a knowledge of osteology. "Marsh was
not only constantly collecting fossils, but also osteological material, and a certain amount of this was . . . coming into the menag-
eries and taxidermists' shops in New York. At Marsh's request, I
devoted much of my spare time to looking about for material of
this kind, which, when desirable, I secured for the [Peabody]
Museum at New Haven. I had always been interested in birds;
had made some collections, and now my association with the
taxidermists led me to continue this work. After a time I got into
the way of having John Wallace — who daily made the rounds of
the New York markets looking for unusual birds — [to] keep me
supplied each day with specimens . . . which I took home and at
night mounted. I kept this up for two or three years, usually
spending two or three hours of the evening down in the cellar,
where I had an excellent outfit for mounting. . . ."[4]

Grinnell was unhappy in his father's firm and longed to return
to the West. Since the epitome of Western adventure was the
buffalo hunt, he wrote Major Frank North in the spring of 1872
to see if this could be arranged. North was unable to go but
suggested his brother, Luther, who agreed. The trip was set for
late summer.

With Jim Russell, Grinnell met North at Elm Creek, Nebraska.
Reboarding a Union Pacific train, the three went on to Plum
Creek where they hired saddle horses, a wagon, and a teamster.
Leaving the tracks, they headed south. Their purpose was to
intercept the Pawnee tribe who a few weeks before had left their
reservation for the summer buffalo hunt. Because of North's long
association with the tribe, as commander of a company of Pawnee
scouts, the party was assured a friendly welcome.

"While on our way to join the Pawnees, in crossing the Platte
River, we almost lost our teamster. We carried our beds, provisions
and mess kit in a wagon hauled by a pair of mules, and driven by
an elderly man who had fought in the Civil War. Full of strange
tales of the perils he had encountered, he was a newcomer on the
plains.

"When we reached the Platte River, which was low and consisted of a bed of sand a mile or a mile and a half wide interrupted by frequent small streams of water, we paused to look for a crossing. Like many western streams, the Platte abounded in quicksand, and wagons were very likely to sink in these sands and to become so firmly embedded that it was difficult to get them out. Lute North had heard from the man at the railroad station that on the bank of the Platte there was a boat or scow used for crossing at times of high water, and it was determined to unload the wagon, put all the property in the boat, and hitching the mules to that to drag it across the river, and then to go back with the mules and cross with the empty wagon, which could be hauled so much more rapidly that there would be less danger of its sinking in the quicksands. We found the boat, loaded it and hitched the mules to it, and then the three riders went ahead, spreading out a little to find a way where the mules could best travel. After a time George, the teamster, started his mules, walking behind them, beside the boat, and very unwisely he walked on its downstream side. Presently, in crossing a channel where the water was deep enough to float the boat, it was swept down against his legs and knocked him down. He fell in the water with a shout, and before we could get to him the loaded boat had gone over most of his body, and only his head was visible. He was clinging to its gunwale, but the boat was steadily working further over him. We galloped back and were able to pull him out, unhurt except for some bruises. Thereafter he walked on the upper side of the boat, which was dragged across the little channels and over the many sand bars, and at last reached the other shore, where it was unloaded, and then taken back to the north bank, where the mules were hitched to the empty wagon. If his companions had been only a little farther away from the team, George would certainly have been drowned."[5]

After the outfit was safely on the south bank of the Platte, the four men continued on their journey. After much hard riding, the expectant buffalo hunters at last reached the Republican River; they knew the Indians could not be far away, for the Republican was on the edge of the buffalo country.

It was now the evening of the third day out, and the party stopped to camp, hoping to catch up with the Pawnees soon after crossing the river the next morning.[6] Waking at dawn, Grinnell describes his unfolding world: "The sun pushing aside the rosy curtains of the east commences to renew his daily course, bringing again light and life to all animated nature. He touches the more elevated bluffs with flaming light and suffuses the whole heavens with a ruddy glow. The leaves of the low willows, frosted with a coating of tiny dew-drops, glisten in his light, and each silvery globule that hangs from the high grass reflects his image like a polished mirror. The waters of the Republican, dark and turbid . . . , seem to become purer as they are touched by his beams, and flash and gleam as they whirl along toward the Missouri. The mellow whistle of the meadow lark is heard from the prairie, the short cry of the migrating blackbird falls from on high, a flock of ducks on whistling wing pass over us on their way to those genial climes where frost and snow do not penetrate, and where the rigors of winter are not felt. . . ."[7]

From what Lute North has told him, Grinnell knows that south of the Republican and north of the Solomon are "many lesser streams, some flowing north and some south. . . . Besides these the plain is intersected by innumerable ravines running in all directions. These serve to carry off the surplus water in times of rain, each emptying into some large one, and that in turn into one still larger, until finally a stream is formed which joins into the main river. On the borders of such streams feed the deer and elk; along the grassy bottoms stalks the wild turkey, resplendent in his bronzed plumage; among the tangled thickets that grow upon their banks lurks the great white wolf; and amid the topmost branches of some lofty cottonwood the white-headed eagle rears her gigantic brood. Among the numberless bluffs that rise one after another like the waves of a tossing sea, the buffaloes [live] . . . by thousands; some peacefully reposing on the rich bottoms, others feeding upon the short nutritious grass that clothes the hillsides. . . .

"Rarely are these scenes disturbed save when the prowling Sioux, returning from some foray upon the luckless settlers, halts for a brief period to rest his worn out animals and to eat his hasty meal, or when a squadron of cavalry with rattle of arms and clink of spur hurries along upon the trail of the dusky robber, all too late to recover his booty or avenge his crimes. A few hunters or a party of surveyors occasionally pass through this region, but except by these and by the Indian it is rarely visited."[8]

Grinnell and his companions are camped on a stream that is "the northern border of the present range of the buffalo. A few passing beyond the Republican advance as far north as the Platte, but rarely cross that river. South of the former, however, they still abound; not in such numbers indeed as in former years, but still often sufficiently numerous to blacken the plains and to become an easy prey to whoever will hunt them." Yet Grinnell knows "their days are numbered," and that "unless some action . . . is speedily taken not only by the States and Territories, but by the National Government, these shaggy brown beasts . . . will ere long be among . . . the things of the past."[9]

Such was Grinnell's perception. When he wrote these words, the wild cattle of the plains still numbered in the millions, and most Americans, including the commercial buffalo hunters, thought they could never be exterminated. Grinnell's prescience was the result of his realization, gained from geology and paleontology, that the land and its life forms are not invulnerable; his reading of Audubon's journals, describing the bison's former abundance and slaughter; and his first-hand acquaintance with the destruction of his own day, as train after train rolled east, their boxcars stuffed with the hides of thousands of buffalo killed by market gunners.[10]

Even more significant than Grinnell's awareness of the bison's plight was his solution for saving the animal. By comprehending the need for a regional approach to this resource problem, through the agency of the federal government, he put himself in the forefront of conservation thought.

It was with a touch of sadness, then, that Grinnell traveled on his way to join the Pawnees, for he had an apprehension that the wild cattle, the wild Indians, and the unspoiled West they represented, were all passing away before his eyes. "When we crossed the Republican and turned southward, the trail . . . we were following became fresher and gave evidence of having been made only the day before. Soon we passed their last night's camp, the ashes of the fires still warm and the fresh buffalo bones not yet dried by the sun. Encouraged by these signs we urged forward our horses, and a short time before dark our exertions were rewarded by the sight of the white lodges of the Pawnees which dotted the broad bottom of Beaver Creek.[11]

"There were about two hundred lodges, occupied by over four thousand Indians, principally Pawnees, with a few Poncas and Omahas. Within the camp and among the lodges were picketed the horses. The reason for this as we afterward learned, was that the Pawnees had encountered that afternoon a small band of Sioux, and after chasing them for several miles had captured four of their horses. Of course they knew that the Sioux, if they had the opportunity, would return the compliment by stampeding their stock and making off with the best of it. This they intended to prevent by keeping the horses so near them that no unusual movement of the herd could be made without being noticed by someone in the camp.

"The scene was one of bustling activity. The women and girls were busily at work bringing water, chopping wood and cooking, while the men strolled about the camp smoking and talking, or clustered together on the bluffs and gazed at us as we approached. Half a mile from the village we halted and made camp and after supper rode over to see old *Peta-la-shar*, the head chief of the Pawnees. He received us courteously, and Lute even warmly, calling him 'my son,' and patting him affectionately on the back as he sat by his side. The old man told us that the hunt so far had not been very successful, that the buffalo were not plenty north of the Republican as they used to be when he was . . . young . . . , but tomorrow, he said, a grand surround would be made, as his young men had reported plenty of buffalo about twenty miles to the southward. Pleased with this intelligence, we left him and after a stroll through the Indian camp returned to our own, and were soon enjoying the deep and dreamless sleep that follows a hard day's march.

"But alas for our anticipations. When we rose next morning we were dismayed by the sight of a dark mist which hung over the valley, sometimes lifting for a few moments so as to disclose the bluffs beyond, and then settling down again heavier than before. It was evident that the scouts sent out by the Indians to look for buffalo would be unable to see through the heavy fog, and so our prospects for a hunt on this day were very poor. We started from our camp soon after the Pawnees moved out, and before long our doleful thoughts were dispelled by the . . . spectacle of four thousand Indians on the march.

"At the head of the column walked eight men, each carrying a long pole wrapped round with red and blue cloth and fantastically ornamented with feathers, which fluttered in the breeze as they were borne along. These were the buffalo sticks, and [they] were religiously guarded at all times, as the success of the hunt was supposed to depend largely upon the respect shown to them. Immediately after these came thirty or forty of the principal men of the tribe, all mounted on superb ponies, their saddles glittering with silver ornaments, and their bridles tinkling with little bells. Then followed a motley assemblage, consisting of the squaws of the tribe, each of whom as she walked along led one or two ponies heavily packed. A moderately loaded pony would carry, first the lodge, with the poles tied on each side of the pack, the ends dragging along on the ground, next a pile of blankets and robes a foot or two in height, around which are tied pots, tin cups, and other utensils, and on top of this heap are perched from two to five small children, each of which holds in its arms two or three . . . puppies. Loose horses without any burdens, and . . . colts, each with a little pack on its back, run at large among . . . the crowd, and their shrill neighings mingle with the barking of the dogs and the incessant clamor of the women. Along the outskirts of this strange concourse ran half a dozen well-grown boys engaged in playing a game in which they seemed intensely interested, and on which as I afterwards learned, they were betting. Each held in his right hand a slender stick about four feet long, and one of them had also a ring of plated rawhide three or four inches in diameter. As the latter ran he threw this ring before him so that it rolled along upon its circumference and then each of the players tried to throw his stick through it. They were not very successful in their attempts, and I fancy that the amounts lost and won were not very heavy. As I cast my eye around over the prairie, I saw on every side small parties of Indians trudging along on foot, their blankets drawn closely about them and their

bows and arrows on their back. Surprised at seeing so many walking when the number of riderless horses in the band was so large,
I asked Lute the reason of it. He told me that they were letting
their horses rest now, so that they might be fresh when they
needed them to run buffalo.

"We travel on for several hours and gradually the mist disap-
pears beneath the powerful rays of the sun. Occasionally we cross
a little stream, and as we approach it forty or fifty men and boys
hurry ahead and disperse themselves through the timber, killing
whatever game they can find. On one occasion a lordly elk disturbed by these invaders, springs from a thicket and runs out
toward the bluffs unfortunately on the wrong side of the creek
and toward the column. Too late he perceives his mistake and
turns to retrace his steps, but is met by a dozen yelling enemies.
Again he turns, and now strives to escape in another direction,
but twenty horsemen have shot out from the main body, and in
less time than it takes to tell it the noble animal is surrounded.
He hesitates, stops, and then makes a bold dash at the weakest
point in the circle, but ere he reaches it three or four arrows
pierce him and he turns again. The circle grows smaller, and
again he makes an effort to break it, but his strength is gone; he
staggers and comes to his knees. Vain are all his efforts; the knife
is at his throat, and with a groan he yields up his life; and in a
few minutes naught remains to mark the spot where the beautiful
creature fell save his horns and a few polished bones that shine
while in the morning sun.

"A little later, distant shouts greet our ears and attract our
attention to another quarter. As we gaze in the direction of the
sounds we see the huge forms of thirty or forty buffalo appearing
over a bluff but a few hundred yards away. Again the better
mounted riders spur out from the line, this time myself among
the number. The buffalo see us, stop, and then separate and flee
in wild confusion. Half a dozen Indians and myself start after
part of them and follow at a full run as they dash madly down a
steep ravine, throwing up dense clouds of dust in their furious
career. As we near the small stream into which the ravine empties,
I am within thirty yards of the hindmost, when a young Indian
mounted on a beautiful, but evidently untrained horse, passes
me and in a few jumps is alongside of the game. He discharges

an arrow, but before he has time to do more, his horse, terrified by the enormous bull, carries him by, and the [bison] ... becomes now the pursuer. I put spurs to my horse, and as soon as I get within easy distance, fire, and the ball entering near the root of the tail ranges diagonally forward and comes out at the shoulder.[12] The huge beast drops to the shot, and I pull up to examine my first buffalo. I marvel at his monstrous size and vast strength, and admire his massive horns and hoofs, which shine like polished ebony, and his shaggy head with its impenetrable shield of hair, hide and bone; and as the Indians prepare to skin the game, I re-mount and ride off, musing sadly upon the future of the Indian and the buffalo.

"As I proceed I am joined by several returning hunters laden with spoil. The red meat neatly sliced from the bones, is piled high behind the riders, and the crimson drops which trickle from it color the flanks of the horses, already wet from their sharp exercises. My companions chatter and laugh in high glee at their success, and we converse as well as we can by means of signs and broken sentences of Pawnee and English. We reach the main body, and the bloody loads are handed over to the squaws and by them transferred to the backs of the much enduring pack animals; the march is resumed and we do not halt again until near noon, when we cross a small creek and prepare to camp. Almost all the company have crossed when we hear a shrill chorus of yells and a great fluttering of wings, and perceive that the foremost of the 'skirmishers' have come upon a band of wild turkeys. Several are killed with clubs, and the rest seek safety, some by running and others by flight. One of the latter passing over us at a height of not more than twenty yards, becomes a target for all the loose articles in the camp. The air is positively darkened by the cloud of arrows, whips, sticks and hatchets that are projected at this unlucky bird. No one seems to care what his missile hits when it comes down, or whether he loses it or not, if he can only get that turkey. The latter sustains no more serious injury than the loss of a few feathers and manages to prolong his flight until he reaches the outskirts of the crowd. There he alights, however, and is immediately pounced upon and torn to pieces by the excited boys.

"All hands having crossed, a spot is chosen where the creek

bottom is wide enough to accommodate the whole company, and camp is made. The animals are unpacked and picketed out to feed; the lodges are set up; a hundred thin columns of smoke denote the existence of as many fires. Some of the squaws hurry away up and down the creek and soon return laden with wood and water, others plant poles upright in the ground and throwing the fresh hides over them commence the tedious operation of scraping off the flesh and fat that still adhere to them. Part of the men ride out toward the bluffs, so as to be the first to receive the news, if anything is reported by the scouts, and a few lounge about our wagon, but by far the greatest number are in their lodges eating their midday meal.

"We had been in camp two hours or more and were lazily reclining under the wagon, when a sudden bustle among the Indians attracted our attention, and on looking out toward the bluffs we saw a horseman riding hard for camp, while the men that he passed shouted and gesticulated in great excitement. On reaching the lodges the rider halted near a group of the chief men and spoke a few words to them. He than rode off again, and after a short consultation some order was given, and in ten minutes the lodges were down and packed and a part of the company were flying off down the creek. Only the women and children, however. While the packing was being done, the men had removed the saddles and bridles from their horses, substituting for the latter a strip of rawhide around the lower jaw. They had also stripped off their own clothing and stood forth as naked as when they came into the world, save for a breech clout and a pair of moccasins apiece. Their bows and arrows they held in their hands. At a given signal they started off, at first on a slow trot, but gradually increasing their speed until the trot became a canter and the canter a swift gallop.

"At the first movement in the camp, Lute had notified us of what would take place, and we had saddled up and leaving all our superfluous articles in the wagon had made ready to start. The wild gallop over the prairie with that excited multitude was an experience calculated to impress itself indelibly upon the memory, and I shall never forget it.

"The band was at first widely scattered, but as we proceeded the ranks closed up, and it became more compact. Many of the Indians leading their horses, advance on foot, keeping well up with the mounted men. Here and there I see two of them mounted on a single horse and leading two others; the former will be turned loose when we approach the buffalo, and its riders will make their hunt on fresh horses.

"On we go, mile after mile, and still no sign of halting. At times the pace is slackened as we ascend some high bluff, and one or two of the leaders cautiously peer over it to see if the game is in sight. In front of the line ride at regular intervals the 'Pawnee Police,' so called, whose duty it is to restrain the more ardent, and those whose horses are fastest, until the charge is made; so that all may have an equal chance at it. Very deliberately they advance, checking their impatient ponies which sniff the chase and are eager to commence it. Sometimes a restive horse carries his rider too far forward and the latter is sternly warned back by the nearest of the leaders. And woe to the luckless [person] . . . that fails to heed such a warning. The power of the 'Police' is absolute during the hunt, and if an order is disobeyed or neglected by the delinquent, be he white or red, of high degree or low, [he] may be knocked off his horse with a club and beaten into submission without receiving any sympathy even from his best friends.

"Six, eight, ten miles have been passed over when a brief halt is made. The game is in sight, and when I ride up to the top of the high bluff where the leaders are congregated, I see on the prairie four or five miles away clusters of dark spots that I know must be the buffalo. Presently we start again and change our course so that a range of bluffs conceals the game. By this time all the Indians have mounted and are pressing as close behind the 'Police' as they dare. The wet flanks of the ponies glisten in the declining sun, and dashes of white foam flake their breasts as with outstretched necks and ears thrown forward they gallop along, showing as much excitement as their riders. The latter sit their animals like Centaurs, their long hair streaming out behind them and lifting at every jump of the horses.

"At length we reach the top of the last ridge and see the buffalo lying down in the creek bottom a mile beyond. The place could not have been more favorable for a surround had it been chosen for that purpose. A plain two miles broad and intersected by a narrow stream, is encircled by high bluffs up which the buffalo must toil slowly, but which the more nimble ponies can ascend almost as fast as they can run on level ground. As we commence to descend the face of the bluff, the pace is slightly accelerated. The Indians at either extremity of the line press forward, and its contour is now crescent-like. Men and horses commence to evince more excitement, but the five hundred buffaloes reposing below us do not seem to notice our advance. A few wiley old bulls, however, that occupy the tops of the lower bluffs, take the alarm and commence to scud off over the hills. At last when we are within half a mile of the ruminating herd, a few of them rise to their feet, and soon all spring up and stare at us for a few seconds; then down go their heads and in a dense mass they rush off toward the bluffs. As they rise to their feet the leaders of our party give the signal, and each man puts his horse to its utmost speed. The fastest horses are soon among the last of the buffalo, but still their riders push forward to try and turn the leaders of the herd and drive them back into the plain. This they in part accomplish, and soon the bottom is covered with the flying animals. They dash madly along and the trained horses keep close to the buffalo without any guidance, yet watch constantly for any indication of an intention to charge, and wheel off if such intention is manifested. The Indians discharging arrow after arrow in quick succession, ere long bring down the huge beasts and then turn and ride off after another."[13] Grinnell rides with them, and bearing down on the herd he kills several while galloping alongside.[14]

In the excitement he fails to notice a charging buffalo cow. She is almost upon him, when, seeing her at last, he violently turns his horse aside. The enraged animal hurls by only inches away.[15] After recovering, he rides to a little hill overlooking the valley to watch the rest of the spectacle. Here he is joined by North and Russell, who have also killed their share. Together, the three white men watch intently, as below them small groups of buffalo are "dashing here and there, closely attended by relentless pursuers."[16]

"Soon the chase is ended, and the plain is dotted with dark objects over each of which bend two or three Indians busily engaged in securing the meat. Every ounce of this will be saved, and what is not eaten while fresh, will be jerked and thus preserved for consumption during the winter. How different would have been the course of a party of white hunters had they the same opportunity. They would have killed as many animals, but would have left all but enough for one day's use to be devoured by the wolves or to rot upon the prairie."[17] Paradoxically, a Stone Age people give the Eastern patrician a valuable lesson in conservation.

"As we ride slowly back, Lute beguiles the way by relating to us some of the traditions of the Pawnees, to which we lend an attentive ear. Camp reached and supper over, we turn our attention to the Indians. There is great rejoicing among the company to-night. Some roast the delicious hump ribs, and some broil the heart and liver. Many stuff the intestines with fragments of the tenderloin and boil them, thus obtaining a most delicate soup, and others take the great marrow bones and greedily feast upon the luscious contents. And so the evening wears away, passed by our little party in the curious contemplation of a phase of life that is becoming more and more rare as the years roll by, and by the Indians in feasting and merriment, and when at last we . . . drop off to sleep, the Pawnees are still [working] . . . away at the buffalo meat. . . ."[18]

Darkness crept over the camp. Outside, on "the plain where the buffalo had fallen, the gray wolf was prowling, and, with the coyote, the fox and the badger, tore at the bones of the slain. When day came, the golden eagle and the buzzard perched upon the naked red skeletons, and took their toll. And far away to the southward, a few frightened buffalo, some of which had arrows sticking in their sore sides, were cropping the short grass of the prairie."[19]

By having the privilege of participating in the Pawnees' summer hunt, Grinnell had an experience few white men had shared. In fact, what he observed would never be seen again on the Great Plains. It was almost as if time had been suspended, for the hunt could easily have taken place thirty or even one hundred years before. The naked Pawnees rode horses without either bridles or saddles, and they used only bows and arrows. There was little in the scene to indicate that these Indians had ever had any contact with the white world. A year later, 156 Pawnees in search of buffalo, most of them women and children, were massacred near the same spot by their ancient enemies, the Sioux. The tribe never went buffalo hunting again.[20]

After a week with his new Indian friends, Grinnell began the return trip to the railroad. Even though at one point during his stay with the Pawnees a band of hostile Indians tried unsuccessfully to run off the horses, he and his companions were unprepared for what was to come. "We had sent off our teamster early in the morning, directing him to drive hard, so as to get across the Republican River, near the mouth of Red Willow Creek, as early as possible and there to camp and give his animals an opportunity to feed. The three of us started somewhat later from the Pawnee camp for the long ride to the Republican, and did not see the wagon until we reached camp that night.

"We had passed over the divide between the Republican and the next stream south, and were traveling down a wide, dry valley. It was well on in the afternoon. The sun was hot, and we were more or less sleepy. No one, I think, except perhaps Lute North, was thinking of anything except the joy of reaching the river and getting to camp. By the merest chance, I happened to turn my head to the left, and looking up a ravine or draw which came down from the low hills perhaps half a mile distant, I saw an Indian on foot, holding to the rope of his horse, and with his right hand raised as if beating the horse about the head, while the horse was pulling back. It was but a moment's glimpse, and I passed a little point of the hill, so that the man had gone out of my sight. I told the others what I had seen. The Indian could not have been a Pawnee, for there were none in that part of the country, all being together at their camp. What seemed likely was that the man I had seen was an enemy — Sioux or Cheyenne — one of those who had attacked the Pawnee camp only a few days before and endeavored to run off the horses.

"From that time on we kept a bright lookout, riding down the middle of the flat valley, far from any cover from which people could shoot. We had gone only a little further when a party of [about fifteen] Indians streamed out from the hills and rode down toward us. Our horses were quite unfit to run, but we hurried them along as fast as possible, but the Indians gained so rapidly that all effort at flight was abandoned. As the most experienced man of the party, Lute North, of course, took the lead. Presently he told us to dismount and bring our horses together in a sort of triangle, and we stood behind them ready to point our guns over the saddles. When they saw us take this position of defense, the Indians halted and seemed to consult a little, and then the greater number began to ride around us in a circle, the diameter of which gradually lessened. The Indians kept themselves pretty well down below their horses' backs. Two or three of them had guns, and from time to time they fired, the bullets usually knocking up the dust long before they reached us, but sometimes singing over our heads, and for a short time the song of each bullet created an extraordinary commotion in my mind, and I experienced the sensation commonly described as 'having your heart in your throat.' This soon passed off, however.

"Some arrows were shot, but none reached us. We had plenty of ammunition, and we wasted little of it, shooting carefully at the men and horses that rode so fast about us. However, the distance was great; the targets moved rapidly, and while on two or three occasions we thought one of us had hit a horse, only one animal was really crippled and that from a shot by North.

"The Indians continued to ride around us for a time. To me it seemed a long time. I suppose as a matter of fact it was perhaps not more than half an hour. They had not much heart in the work, for the chances were all against them. They were poorly armed, and we had the best guns of that day. Besides that, they no doubt knew, what we did not, that near the mouth of the Red Willow, on the Republican, was camped a troop of cavalry. It was always possible that some of these troops might ride in this direction and hear the shooting, in which case they would follow the Indians.

"After a time, the Indians stopped riding around us and gathered at a distance, where they discussed matters, and while they were doing this we remounted and went on our way. Twice more the Indians stopped us, but with no result further than the delay, and the last time we moved on they were still grouped together on the prairie, no doubt soon to ride away into the hills."[21] The aborigines who attacked the white party were probably Cheyennes, members of the same tribe Grinnell would later definitively study.[22]

"That night when we reached the Republican we reported what happened to Lieutenant Smead, who was in command there, but there was nothing . . . he could do. We slept in a dugout, the prey of a multitude of mosquitoes of unparalleled fierceness, and the next day followed down the valley of the Republican. . . .[23]

"Even then there were settlers in the valley . . ., and I recall very well one man who had built himself a house of cottonwood logs, broken up a piece of ground, and had a respectable corn patch — of course unfenced. This man devoted much of the time we were with him to anathematizing the buffalo, which on frequent occasions came to his cornfield and fed on the tender stalks. He told us of a buffalo bull that he had killed that spring, which was wholly blind, its eyes apparently having been put out by a prairie fire. The bull was old, but perfectly able to get about, and had not yet been attacked by wolves. It was cross . . . and would not run when he tried to drive it, but instead charged in the direction of the sound."[24]

It was after leaving the Republican River and heading north to the Platte that Grinnell and his friends again were threatened, though not attacked, by a Cheyenne war party. The Indians followed behind the whole day, but left in the evening when the whites luckily happened to meet some Fort McPherson officers out hunting.[25] Years later, Grinnell reminisced about the incident in a letter to Lute North: "We might very well have got in [to] trouble on that occasion, though . . . at the time I did not know enough to realize the . . . danger. I remember . . . how you drove old George and hurried up our trip in to the river."[26]

The 1872 buffalo hunt "was . . . thoroughly enjoyed by [the] young men from 22 to 25 . . ., who had already had a taste of frontier life and [who] had become . . . fond of it."[27] For Grinnell, the trip was cheap as well as enjoyable. "Horace F. Clark and Augustus Schell gave me passes over the New York Central and Hudson River Railroad, the Lake Shore, Chicago and Northwestern, and Union Pacific Railroads. They even gave me a pass on the sleeping car, so that my trip to western Nebraska, even though I traveled in [the] most luxurious fashion, was highly inexpensive."[28] For so little, he had been able to travel two thousand miles and ten thousand years, from the sumptuous dining car of a late-nineteenth-century train to the wilderness campfire of a Stone Age people — and back — all in a three-week summer vacation.

During their buffalo hunt, Lute North and Grinnell became

fond of each other, and the friendship would last their lifetimes. Before separating on the train, as North headed for his home in Nebraska and Grinnell for New York, they agreed to have another hunt next summer, this time for elk.

When August of 1873 arrived, both men were ready. "Starting out at a point on the . . . [Union] Pacific Railroad, about one hundred and fifty miles west of Omaha, a party of three [composed of Grinnell, North, and the teamster], we pulled out on the afternoon of the last day of August, on a march toward the Loup."[29] The men were somewhat apprehensive of the trip, since the trail along the river was sometimes used by the Sioux when on their raids. Uppermost in the minds of Grinnell and North was the already mentioned massacre of Pawnees by Sioux which had taken place only a few weeks before.

To the young Easterner, Lute North was "my *guide*, philosopher, and friend."[30] He had already taught Grinnell much about the West, and in the summers ahead this amiable student-teacher relationship would continue. The teamster was Jack Robinson, "an excellent and amusing fellow, [who] sat in the wagon containing our provisions and bedding, behind his rattling team of sorrels, that trotted along at a pace [which] . . . promised well for a speedy arrival at the hunting grounds."[31]

North had already told Grinnell: " 'I can promise to give you at least a shot at . . . elk, but [I] don't know whether you'll kill or not. They're pretty good game. Not many men around here can say that they've killed an elk.' "[32] This last statement worried Grinnell, for he was afraid that when the time came, he would get "elk fever" and miss his target.

"We traveled about twenty miles the first day and camped on a small creek where we found wood and water. A little fried bacon, some biscuits hastily cooked, and a cup of coffee constituted our first meal in camp, and after smoking a quiet pipe we lie down by the fire. Lute's last observation is, 'We'll have game to-morrow night, boys.' My heart gives a throb, and I secretly pray that I may be the one to kill it.[33]

"We started with the sun the next morning and had a long day's march. Lute and [I] . . . hunted through the ravines, while the wagon kept on the divide. We saw no game except three deer, which jumped up about seventy-five yards from Lute. Shooting from his horse, he touched one of them in the hind leg, but not seriously, as we watched it for a long distance and though it fell behind the others, it kept up a gait we knew would carry it away from our ponies, fast though they were.

"We had traveled all day, and were hot and tired when we came to a creek where there was good camping ground. The sun was only about two hours above the western horizon, and we decided to camp as soon as a place could be found where we could get the horses down to the water. In looking for such a place Lute rode toward the top of a little ridge to get a wider view. Suddenly I saw him bend down over the neck of his horse and wheeling around gallop toward us. 'There they are, boys,' he cried, 'elk, about twenty of them.' In a moment we were all excitement, and were hastily following his hurried directions. The horses were unhitched and unsaddled, and picketed out. Firearms and knives were examined, and we descended into the bed of the creek, whence the elk had just emerged about half a mile further up. . . .

"Who can describe the labor of our advance on that band of elk? . . . I can only say that the bed of the creek was full of water and very miry, that the sides were nearly perpendicular, and were almost everywhere covered with a thick growth of nettles, briers, and creeping plants; where bare they were wet and very slippery; that the sun was blazing down as only a Nebraska sun can blaze, and that we ran ahead when we could, and fell ahead when we couldn't run. Fortunately there was no wind; . . . for the elk's sense of smell is so acute that it is more to be feared by the hunter than its powers of vision.

"At last we were within three hundred yards of the place where the game was supposed to be, and it behooved us to move cautiously. Lute carefully ascended the bank and looked about. . . . For a long time he gave no sign, but at length I saw him lower his head and creep rapidly toward us. 'They are moving,' he whispered, 'feeding along toward the bluffs; we must hurry.' As fast as possible we hastened up the creek, and soon, after another look by our leader, turned up a ravine. The utmost caution was now necessary. We crawled along, not on our hands and knees, but flat on our faces for some distance, Lute first, myself next and Jack last. Presently we turned and commenced to ascend the side of the ravine, and as we neared the ridge Lute stopped and motioned me up beside him. 'They're just over the ridge. Crawl up and take the first shot.' I feebly resisted, but he reiterated the order, and I complied. On reaching the top I cautiously raised my head, and there within a hundred yards of me I saw the ears of an old cow elk. The sight was almost too much for me, and I sank back a moment. Then steadying my nerves by a violent effort, I raised my old Sharpe. Carefully with finger on trigger, I full-cocked it, and sighted where Lute had told me . . ., about eight inches behind the fore shoulder and low down. For a moment I could not hold well on her, for the flies troubled her and she kept moving, but at last she stood still, and I pulled. The smoke hid her from me, and I sprang forward just as Lute ran by me, to get a shot at the herd as they fled. In a moment I was at his side, and we stopped just about where my cow had stood when I fired. The elk were running briskly off about half a mile away; none of them seemed to be wounded, and I could see nothing of the one at which I had fired. At that moment I felt particularly small. Suddenly Lute shouted, 'There she is,' and following the direction of his glance, I saw a movement in the short prairie grass. We rushed to the spot, and there lay the cow, kicking in her death agony. My ball had passed through her heart, and she had run about fifty yards before falling. That was for me the supreme moment. As I stood over her, all the trouble and annoyance of the trip, all the worries and cares of everyday life were forgotten, and I was absorbed in the proud contemplation of the graceful creature lying before me.

"Lute was cordial in his congratulations. 'I knew that you hit her,' he said, 'for I crawled up behind you and saw that you held steady as a rock.'

"After bleeding and butchering our game, we started for camp. It was now almost dark, for it had taken us quite two hours to reach the place where we then were. Striking off over the prairie, we arrived at our camp in about fifteen minutes, and after a delightful supper spent an hour or two talking over the incidents of the day, and listening to Lute's stories of hunts and Indian fights. . . .

"Early next morning we were afoot, and before night the flesh of the elk, neatly stripped from the bones, was in [the] process of being jerked. For five days we hunted with most satisfying results. Elk [were] . . . found and killed on several occasions. Finally, forced to it by 'the terror by night,' viz., mosquitos, we turned our faces homeward. On the last day but one of our return march, we camped early and rode out to take a last look for game. As we descended the slope of a high bluff, Lute's eye, which was constantly roving along the horizon, caught sight of some moving objects just appearing over the top of another bluff a few hundred yards off. Crouching low in our saddles we galloped down into the ravine, and, leaving our horses, ascended the next ridge, whence the elk could be seen feeding slowly toward us. We had only to wait until they came within shot. Very deliberately they advanced, the leaders, two fine bulls, stopping every now and then to look, smell, or listen, and then boldly stepping forward, as if to encourage the more timid females and young. Had we waited I am confident that they would have come up within ten yards of us. It would have been little else than murder, however, to have shot them so near, and I was glad to see Lute look around at us and signal . . . to be ready, while they were still more than a hundred yards distant. The three rifles cracked almost simultaneously, but to our chagrin only one animal fell. It was Lute's bull. Jack and I had fired too hastily, and had missed. As the herd swept round the hill, in full flight, we fired again, but with no better result. A third shot from Jack as they were ascending the bluffs brought down a large bull, and as they were about to disappear, I raised my two hundred and fifty yard sight and carefully fired at a large cow which ran a little behind the others. As I lowered my rifle I saw her stagger, and then, turning off to one side, move down a ravine on three legs. Running back to the horses I sprang into the saddle and urged forward my pony with whip and spur. I was soon within sight of the cow, which, although on three legs, ran very fast, and I had ridden nearly two miles before I got close enough to shoot from the saddle with any certainty of killing. At last, however, I fired while on a run and brought her down, but it took another shot to finish her. It was an exciting chase, and I did not realize until I passed over the ground on my return what a mad gallop it had been. I had ridden through sloughs so miry that on reaching them

again I was [obliged] . . . to pick out a better crossing; [and] had
descended on a full run the sides of cañons so steep that I now
preferred leading my horse up to riding him. . . .

"We had now plenty of work on hand. The heads and skins
were prepared for mounting, the meat jerked, and with a wagon
heavily loaded we started for the railroad."[34] The party reached
the Union Pacific line without incident, and a few days later
Grinnell was back in New York.

4

Exploring With Custer

THE YOUNG PATRICIAN returned to new responsibilities as a business man. In the spring of 1873, "my father's partner, Horace F. Clark, a son-in-law of Cornelius Vanderbilt, died. This was a dreadful misfortune to my father, who admired and loved Mr. Clark. Clark, Schell, and Bancker were then three large stock operators, and the first two great railroad men. They thoroughly believed in their enterprises and had loaded up with many thousand shares of stock, which my father's firm was carrying for them on a margin.[1] So long as Mr. Clark was living, any additional margin required was always forthcoming. The stocks had recently been appreciating in price, and there was no thought but that they would go much higher. My father retired September 1, 1873, turning the business over to Joseph C. Williams, who had long been the firm's cashier, and to me, under the title George Bird Grinnell & Co. . . .

"About the middle of September, efforts were made to obtain from Schell, Bancker and the estate of Horace F. Clark additional margin on the very large amount of stock that we were carrying

[78]

for them, but nothing came of these efforts. Commodore Vanderbilt, who might have helped, did not like James H. Bancker, and Mr. Schell was not very active in his efforts to procure the securities.

"The panic of 1873 came on out of a clear sky, about September 20th. Trusted officers of banks and corporations disappeared with the money of the institutions; the stock market promptly fell to pieces; prices dropped almost to nothing; and the Stock Exchange, to put a period to the ruin that seemed impending, closed its doors.[2]

"Meantime my father had come to the aid of the new firm with money and influence. Every effort was made to secure the support of the customers for whom we were carrying the stock, but they failed to respond, and the result was that the new firm failed. Two or three suits were begun to throw it into bankruptcy, with the fortunate result that it was impossible for money lenders, who held stocks as security, to sell them out. The panic being checked by the closing of the Stock Exchange and by these suits, time was given for businessmen to regain their equilibrium; the market began to recover and people to take measures to protect themselves.

"The winter was one of great suffering for the family, and in my efforts to divert my mind from the misfortune that had happened, I began to write short hunting stories for . . . *Forest and Stream*, a newspaper which had been established the previous August, and to which, on the strength of a sample copy, I had subscribed. These little stories, the first of which was published in October, 1873, and dealt with my recent Nebraska elk hunt, I took to the office of *Forest and Stream*, in Fulton Street, myself. There I met Barnet Phillips, Capt. John Taylor, and somewhat later Charles Hallock [editor], and thus began an acquaintance with *Forest and Stream* which lasted for forty years.

"During the winter the legal proceedings against G. B. Grinnell & Co. and George Bird Grinnell and Co. were dismissed; our customers took some of their stocks off our hands, and the concern resumed with money enough to pay all its debts and to have a little capital remaining. My father, having brought us safely out of the woods, retired to Audubon Park. After he had gone, there was nothing to hold me to Wall Street, and I had always had a settled dislike for the business."[3] Since the 1870 expedition, Grinnell and O. C. Marsh had been in continual communication concerning their mutual scientific interests, and more than once the paleontologist had suggested that Grinnell pursue graduate studies at Yale. At last he made up his mind to declare his independence of his father. Despite the latter's disappointment, Grinnell dissolved the firm of George Bird Grinnell & Co. in March, 1874, and went to New Haven to work in the Peabody Museum as one of Marsh's assistants.[4]

At the time "there was no college or Museum fund out of which I could be paid, and for three years I worked without pay, living as economically as I could. The first year I spent $535, the second year $637.50.

"In the late spring of 1874 Gen. [Philip H.] Sheridan wrote Professor Marsh that during the summer an expedition would be sent to the Black Hills of Dakota, and . . . that Professor Marsh might, if he wished, send with it a man to collect fossils."[5] The Army was continuing to play its new role as the subsidizer of the more sophisticated, academic approach to Western exploration. "Professor Marsh asked me to go. I was qualified as a collector and had some knowledge of North American birds and mammals. . . . I took with me L. H. North, as assistant.[6] On my way West I stopped in Chicago and saw General . . . Sheridan, then a young and active man. He gave me the necessary orders, and sent me on to St. Paul, where I reported to Capt. William Ludlow, Chief Engineer of the Department of Dakota, and met North. A day or two later we left St. Paul for Fargo, where we spent the night, and the following day took a daylight train for Bismarck, Dakota, just across the river from Fort Abraham Lincoln, our destination. At that time Bismarck was the end of [the] track for the Northern Pacific Railroad, which ran a daily train, by daylight only, to Fargo. From that point west trains ran to Bismarck every other day, going one day and returning the next."[7] On boarding the train, Grinnell and North met the commander of the expedition: George Armstrong Custer.[8]

"The day after reaching Bismarck, Capt. North and I went over to the post, where quarters were assigned us, and where we remained for over three weeks before the expedition started. At the post I met most of the officers of the 7th Cavalry and a number of those of the 15th and 22nd Infantry. The sutlers were Colonel Wilson and Major Dickey of Bismarck, and the sutler's clerk, W. Parkin, afterward became well-known in the region. He married a half-breed woman, a daughter of the French trader, Picotte, and they had a large stock ranch and store on the Cannonball River."⁹

Grinnell also met "Lonesome" Charley Reynolds, so-called "because he preferred to go off and hunt or trap by himself rather than to spend his time in the dreary little frontier towns where cards and whiskey were the sole diversion."¹⁰ Until his death two years later at the Little Bighorn, Reynolds would be Grinnell's dearest friend. He was Custer's chief scout, and Grinnell, Lute North, and others who would have long experience in the West considered him to be the most competent scout and hunter they ever encountered.¹¹

"At the time of our trip to the Black Hills Charley was thirty-one years old. . . . He was born in western Kentucky, somewhere within 100 miles of Memphis, Tenn. His father was a gentleman, well-to-do, and fond of outdoor sports, among other things a great deer hunter, following his hounds on horseback over the rough mountains near his home. He had been a slave owner. When Charley was a little fellow about twelve or fourteen years old, he was sent away to boarding school, to Indianapolis, Ind. An uncle of his lived in that city. His stay there was not long. He was homesick, and was, as he imagined, unjustly treated by the principal of the school, and before long he ran away. He did not dare . . . go home nor to his uncle, but determined to depend on himself for support, and started west on foot. . . .

"In some way he joined an emigrant train going across the plains, and traveled with it to what is now Denver, where the train disbanded, and he was thrown on his own resources. He had a little money, given him perhaps for his services while crossing the plains, and this enabled him to buy a little pistol and to support himself for a short time. Before very long, however, his money gave out. There was no opportunity for him to get anything to do in Denver, and he started to walk further into the mountains to see if he could get employment somewhere. He was now about fifteen or sixteen years old.

"He walked for a day and a half into the hills without eating anything, and began to get pretty hungry and pretty desperate. One evening he came to a little cabin, and made up his mind that here he would eat. He entered and drew his . . . pistol from his holster, and, pointing it at the man who was getting supper there, ordered him to give him something to eat at once. The . . . old man looked at him with a queer smile, but said nothing, and set food before him, and Charley put his pistol down by the side of the plate and burst out crying. The old fellow spoke kindly and pleasantly to him, and after Charley had eaten drew from him his story. He kept the boy with him all that winter and through the following year, taught him much about hunting, trapping and mountain life, and purchased for him a . . . rifle. Very likely Charley would have remained with him for a long time, but the next summer the old man died and the boy was thrown adrift again. However, his experiences had taught him something about taking care of himself, and thereafter he was never in great straits.

"In the later '60's Charley was on the Missouri hunting and trapping, and from about 1868 to 1872 Fort Berthold was his headquarters, and the Missouri between that and Bismarck and the Little Missouri River were his chief hunting and trapping grounds. He was a remarkable shot with a rifle and a good trapper. His success in hunting, he told me, came largely from the fact that he strove to learn in every possible way — by reading and by observation in the field — the ways of the animals . . . he hunted. The Rees, Mandans and village Gros Ventres of the Berthold Agency believed that he possessed some special medicine, which when used, induced the animals to come to him. On one or two occasions they talked of killing him because his success in hunting was so great. They were especially exercised about some natural history books . . . he used to read, and believed the pictures in these books exerted some influence on the deer, elk, antelope and buffalo. Peter Beauchamp, a half-breed Ree, . . . has told me . . . something of the way in which these Indians regarded Charley. Peter was for a number of months hired by

Charley to keep camp for him, look after stock, and so on.

"Almost immediately after Gen. Custer assumed command at Fort Lincoln he heard of Reynolds and of his remarkable qualifications as scout and hunter, and in a very short time he succeeded in securing his services as chief of scouts at the post.... It was in 1874, on the Black Hills expedition, that I had the opportunity of learning something of his great knowledge of the habits of animals, the Indians and generally of prairie life.

"From some cause or other we were detained at [Fort] Lincoln for nearly thirty days after the date which was originally set for the expedition's departure...."[12] "At the post were a number of newspaper correspondents, among them one representing the *New York Herald*, another the *Tribune* ..., and another the *St. Paul Pioneer Press.* ... The correspondents wrote frequent letters which were published in the East, and which stirred up in many people a wish to accompany the expedition to the Black Hills.... Custer complained that he was overwhelmed with mail applications ..., and not a few men came to the post insisting that they should go along in various capacities. One of these men, finding that he could go in no other way, secured a position as additional clerk to John Smith, the sutler of the expedition."[13]

"During this time there came to the post, without any letters, a Frenchman who stated that he was a scientific man and wished to accompany the expedition. Gen. Custer explained to him that he could not be taken along except by order of Gen. Sheridan, and the man when he heard this became very much excited and declared that he would go to the Black Hills anyhow. About noon the next day it developed that the man had started from Fort Lincoln soon after daylight, and had walked up over the bluffs in a southwesterly direction. The country was bad, for Indians sometimes rode up to the edge of the bluffs above the post, and no one supposed that the man could go twenty miles without being picked up by some wandering war party. However, Charley saddled up, found the trail of the man who had gone afoot, set off and overtook him nearly thirty miles from the post. He was apparently crazy, was walking rapidly in a southwesterly direction, talking to himself in an unknown tongue and gesticulating violently. He refused to stop when Charley overtook him, and in fact probably did not understand a word that Reynolds said, any more than Charley understood him. However, after a long wrangle Charley induced the man to turn about with him, and, mounting him on his own horse, walked beside him, and reached the post about daylight the following day. The man was put in the hospital under guard and before long was sent East. Anyone who knows anything about tracking will understand that to follow the trail of a man on foot for twenty or twenty-five miles is not an easy matter."[14]

"During our stay at Ft. Lincoln, I occupied myself in collecting bird skins, for the bottoms of Heart River and the Missouri River, and on the high, dry prairie adjacent, were very favorable collecting grounds. The season was too late for the best results, since all the birds were breeding. Occasionally Lute North and I went hunting, sometimes alone, and sometimes in company with Charley Reynolds and [Horatio Nelson] Ross, an old miner and prospector who with [William T.] McKay was to prospect in the Black Hills, by direction of Gen. Custer.

"During the wait at Lincoln, I was occasionally at . . . Custer's house, where the General delighted to relate his hunting exploits, and where Mrs. Custer was extremely kind and hospitable. At the various officers' quarters, and also in the billiard room of the sutlers' store, I frequently met officers of the regiments who were stationed at Forts Yates, Sully and Rice. Among these were [Lieutenant Frank M.] Gibson, . . . [Captain] Myles Moylan, and many others of the 7th Cavalry. Lieut. [Donald] McIntosh I did not meet until the expedition started. In appearance he was a full-blooded Indian, and it was said [he] was the son of a Hudson Bay factor in Canada by a St. Regis Indian woman. He was reported to be one of the first authorities in the country on military law. He was a particularly quiet and kindly man, with perfect manners.

"Other men who were on the expedition were Gen. Geo. A. (Sandy) Forsyth and Col. Fred D. Grant, son of Gen. [Ulysses S.] Grant. . . . 'Sandy' Forsyth was looked up to with enormous respect, because in 1868 he had been in command at the Beecher Island fight on the Arikaree Fork of the Republican River, where he had been three times wounded."[15] Forsyth and his men had been attacked by a huge party of Cheyenne, Arapaho and Sioux; some accounts claim as many as nine hundred. The whites crossed to a sand island in the river which they later named Beecher Island, after First Lieutenant Frederick Beecher who was killed on the first day. Even though the soldiers were greatly outnumbered, they had seven-shot repeating rifles and managed to hold off the Indians for several days. The scouts Forsyth sent out got through, and a detachment of the 10th Cavalry finally came to their rescue. Forsyth had six of his men killed and seventeen wounded; he claimed the soldiers had killed thirty-two of the aborigines, though Grinnell, after talking with the Cheyennes years later, reduced that figure to nine.[16]

"Owing to circumstances," Forsyth's "wounds received no attention for two weeks or so, and when he recovered it was discovered that the leg which had been broken was an inch shorter than the other. He went to a hospital in Philadelphia; had his leg rebroken and stretched, and when he was again afoot, it was found that he was still lame. The broken leg was too short. A third time he had it broken and stretched, and this time the operation was successful. It required some pluck to go through all this. This story I did not learn from him; it came out years afterward in connection with inquiries made about him."[17]

At last, the expedition was ready to set out on its sixty day exploration of the mysterious Black Hills. Because of expected trouble with hostile Indians, the military command was a large one, consisting of ten companies of 7th Cavalry, two companies of Infantry, and·a battery of three Gatling guns. The scientific staff included, in addition to Ludlow, Grinnell and North, the state geologist of Minnesota, N. H. Winchell, his assistant, A. B. Donaldson, chief medical officer and botanist, Dr. J. W. Williams, and W. H. Wood, civilian assistant to Captain Ludlow. "There was a wall tent for each pair of men, and we messed together, having our own cook.

"With the outfit were 40 or 50 schoolboys from the Santee Sioux Indian school, who were supposed to act as scouts. They were uniformed and armed by the Government. There were 25 or 30 Arikara Indians from Ft. Berthold, of whom Bloody Knife and Bear's Ears were the principal men.[18] There was also present a man named Two Crows . . . , who in 1890 was the chief priest of the Arikaras. Bear's Ears was an oldish man, who was reported to have led a life of some adventure. As a young man he had fallen in love with a girl who had been promised to an older and more important man. Bear's Ears tried to kill this rival, but failed . . . and was himself wounded and obliged to run away from the tribe. He took refuge with some band of Sioux — [or] possibly Cheyennes — and devoted many years in an effort to secure revenge on his enemy. After I came to know him well, he confided to me that the three fingers gone from his left hand had been offered up in sacrifice to the powers, to secure their help in accomplishing his purpose. The sacrifice was evidently effective, because it was related of Bear's Ears that he finally succeeded in killing his enemy, and when he had done that he further gratified his revenge by eating a portion of the enemy's heart.

"The Ree scouts were disposed to be very friendly to me because of my close association with Lute North. Lute talked Pawnee fluently, and this was a passport to the good graces of all the Rees. I knew half a dozen words of Pawnee and was supposed to know much more. Lute once overheard two of the Indians talking about me, and one informed the other that I could talk good Pawnee — as well as my companion."[19]

The great column of twelve hundred men and their horses, wagons and beef herd left Fort Lincoln at 8:00 A.M. on July 2. A sixteen-piece band mounted on white horses preceded it playing "Garry Owen," Custer's favorite tune.[20] Heading southwest, the reconnaissance had two basic goals. The first was to explore unmapped Indian country with the idea of finding possible locations for a fort.[21] This might seem like a reasonable objective for a military expedition, except that the Black Hills, by treaty, belonged to the Sioux. The other objective was to investigate rumors of gold.[22] To further this end, Custer brought with him the two prospectors whose ore samples could be tested in the field by Winchell, the geologist.[23]

The region through which the whites would travel "had never been traversed by wagons, and there was no such thing as a road. Old Louis Agard was the guide, so called, and there were two or three Sioux from the Hunk-pa-pa band who camped at or near the Standing Rock Agency at Fort Yates. One of these was named Cold Hand, a cripple who walked with a stick, and another was Goose. The latter was alive as late as 1902, when on the occasion of my being at Standing Rock Agency he stopped me near the store, asking me if I had not gone to the Black Hills with Yellow Hair [Custer] a good many years ago. I was much astonished that he should apparently have remembered my face after 28 years.

"The Indian scouts were all under the supervision of Second Lieutenant [George D.] Wallace, who had just graduated from West Point. He was a very tall, awkward young man, but a delightful fellow, much interested in his work, and [he] gave every promise of becoming a splendid soldier. He was killed at the Wounded Knee fight in 1890, the same year that poor Ned Casey, who had been at school with me in Sing Sing [Churchill Military School], was killed by the Sioux."[24]

The expedition crossed the north fork of the Cannonball River, then the south fork (Cedar Creek), the north fork of the Grand, and on July 14 came into "a well grassed and watered valley, through which flowed a small wooded branch of the Little Missouri. The view here was so attractive, in comparison with the landscape recently passed over, that General Custer named the place Prospect Valley."[25] Here the column halted, and the men and animals rested after a 230-mile march. The camp lay between two ranges of pine-clad hills, and sixty miles to the south the Black Hills could be plainly seen as they rose darkly up from the prairie floor. Grinnell and Winchell spent the day searching for fossils. The first of these "bug hunters," as the scientists were called by the military, made a discovery so interesting that Custer momentarily forgot his quest for gold.[26] In a dispatch, he enthusiastically reported: "Mr. Grinnell of Yale College . . . discovered . . . yesterday an important fossil; it was a bone about four feet long and twelve inches in diameter and had evidently belonged to an animal larger than an elephant."[27]

Whether excavating fossils or gathering firewood, every man under Custer had to do a full day's work — and the days began early. "Reveille was usually sounded at 4:00, breakfast was ready at 4:30, and by 5:00 tents were down and wagons packed, and the command was on the march. Usually, unless there was some special purpose for going off to one side, we rode with headquarters, which consisted of the commanding officer, his staff, the chief of the scouts [Reynolds], and various unattached persons who were not in the military service. At a distance of half a mile or so followed the cavalry; after them came the wagons and — to one side — the beef herd, while the infantry brought up the rear. The Indian scouts usually went far ahead and on both flanks of the command, covering much country."[28]

Descending into the valley of the Little Missouri, Grinnell and Winchell found more valuable fossils, including those of two giant turtles. The command camped on the river's bank on July 16.

"After we had been out 15 or 20 days and the country began to be considered dangerous because of possible hostile Indians, orders were given that no one should go away from the column for any purpose, except by special permission from the commanding officer. This order, of course, was not always obeyed. I recall an occasion when I was riding with headquarters when, as we passed over a ridge, a man on foot was seen half a mile ahead, apparently trying to approach some game. The man at first did not see the headquarter command, which Gen. Custer halted. Calling up Reynolds, he said to him, 'Reynolds, bring that man in.' Charley inquired, 'Do you want me to go and get him General?' 'No,' said the General, 'Shoot at him and bring him in in that way.' Charley stepped out and elevating his sights fired a shot in the direction of the man, and a little later a puff of dust rose from the plain just beyond him. The hunter faced about and stared, and Reynolds was ordered to shoot again, which he did, and the man started on a run toward the command. When he got there, he was put under arrest and sent to the rear for disobedience.... The man declared that Charley Reynolds was the most wonderful shot in the world, and showed a place in his hair where he said a lock had been cut away by one of the bullets. He was greatly impressed by Reynolds' ability to shoot as close to him as that and still ... miss him. Of course he knew that there was no intention of hitting him. As a matter of fact, Reynolds shot well over the man on each occasion and took care that the ball should not go near him."[29]

Custer's order that no one could leave the main body of the column did not apply, of course, to the scouts; nor did it include the scientists or those who were expected to supply the camp with game. The side trips Grinnell and North were continually making for the purpose of collecting fossils and natural history notes combined hunting whenever the opportunity arose.

"The country through which we passed was full of game. There were no buffalo, though it was apparent that they had been there in the spring, but antelope were everywhere in extraordinary numbers. About many of the bluffs and tall buttes which we passed there were great numbers of black-tailed deer, and as we drew near the Hills, bear sign became rather common.[30] The company never suffered for lack of fresh meat.

"During this trip I made a very peculiar shot at an antelope, which I have often told of, without greatly considering my reputation for veracity. With three or four Ree scouts I was riding ahead of the command, and when we came to a hill which seemed to overlook considerable territory, we scattered out and went up at different points, the men being perhaps 100 yards apart. When I looked over the hill I saw immediately before me, and perhaps 75 yards distant, a buck antelope, at which — without very much thought — I fired, and the antelope fell. On going up to it, I discovered [that] its four legs were broken, and then [I] examined it with some care. The ball had entered the left side, just back of the shoulder, and so low down that it had chipped a piece of bone out of the olecranon, or point of the elbow. It had gone through the animal's body, broken the humerus, turned at right angles, cut through four or five ribs about half way up the side, broken the right femur, turned again at right angles, and struck the left hock of the antelope so severe a blow that it had unjointed the hock, the foot hanging to the joint by a little thread of skin as large as a piece of ordinary brown wrapping twine. Close to the animal's hind legs I picked up the rifle ball, flattened out to the size of half a dollar, quite circular, but, of course, thicker in the middle than at the edges. If I had not had much experience with the eccentricities of rifle balls, I think I should not have believed this story if anyone had told it to me as having happened to himself."[31]

As indicated earlier, the fact that Grinnell was a good friend of Lute North meant that he was quickly accepted by the Rees who accompanied the expedition. "An evidence of kindly feeling shown by a Ree, whose name I do not know, was displayed during a long march when no water was to be had. We had left camp very early in the morning, and it was known that we would not reach a camping place until late at night. The sun was hot and everyone suffered from thirst. Toward the end of the day . . . North and I were riding along through a wide, dry valley when we heard behind us a faint call, and looking back saw an Indian trying to attract our attention and holding up to view something that glittered in the sun. We were in no mood to ride back to him, nor even to wait, and went on, to be presently overtaken by the Indian, who offered us a canteen of water and explained to Lute that he had ridden twelve miles off the trail to a spring he knew of to get this water for our benefit." [32]

Continuing south, the expedition crossed the Belle Fourche River on the edge of the Black Hills on July 18. "As the command drew near the . . . Hills and crossed the north fork of the Big Cheyenne River — called by the Cheyennes Bear Creek — the way became rougher, and progress more slow. Now, too, the livestock began to suffer. The horses and mules had been fed grain all winter and for the first few weeks of the trip, but now the grain was exhausted, and they had only the prairie grass to eat. The Indian ponies throve on this, but not so the American horses and mules. Before long a good many of the cavalrymen were walking and their horses were being driven along with the beef. When a horse failed and could no longer keep up, he was killed." [33]

On July 20 the command entered the Black Hills. "Lute North and I were mounted on a couple of old, condemned cavalry horses, which were just about able to carry us. As the road grew worse, the strain on the animals was greater. Sometimes, starting soon after 4 o'clock in the morning, camp was not reached until 8 o'clock at night, sometimes not till midnight, and sometimes not at all. The units of the expedition stopped wherever they might be to eat and sleep. It might take two or three days to get the column closed up." [34]

As the terrain changed from prairie and badlands to pine-covered mountains, the fauna underwent a corresponding transformation. Deer now replaced antelope as the most numerous big-game animal, and on several days the expedition's hunters killed one hundred or more. Using new Winchester repeaters, Grinnell and his companion got their share: "Almost every day Captain North and I came into camp with a deer on the saddle, and when, as several times happened, we had traveled until after dark with no signs of camp or of the command catching up, we stopped at some little spring or brook, picketed our animals, made a meal of deer meat, and slept there, wrapped in our saddle blankets. . . ."[35] The next morning they would rejoin the reconnaissance.

Though the day began in a routine way, Sunday, July 26, would prove to be a memorable date for all the members of the expedition. "The clear notes of the bugle sounding 'Stables' aroused us, and before we put on our shoes and trousers and rolled up our beds, the cook shouted breakfast.[36] The sun was just rising, but it was very cold and most of us stood shivering about the fire with our plates in our hands and our tin cups of coffee on the ground beside us while we ate our breakfast. By the time this was over the tents were down, the wagons driven up to load, and our horses saddled.

"Before 'Boots and Saddles' were sounded, Charley Reynolds and Ross rode up and asked Lute and myself if we did not wish to ride with them and make a little hunt.[37] We were not loathe [sic] and soon the four of us were starting off up the valley intending to cross over a low ridge through the timber, and see if we could not kill something for both messes. The weather was bitter[ly] cold, and the frost had shrivelled up all the beautiful flowers which spangled the green valley. No game was seen in crossing through the timber, nor did we meet with anything in the next valley.

"I rode with Charley and Lute with Ross, but although we searched carefully for game none was seen until the morning was well along, and then a single deer was observed at the edge of some distant timber. It was too far off for a sure shot, and presently it disappeared in the brush without being shot at. After a time we halted to smoke, and here we made a little fire and warmed ourselves. We traveled quite a long distance over the hills and through the brush, and at last bent around and returned to the trail where headquarters and the troops had passed. Here we halted again and built a fire and slept through until the wagons came up.

"When we reached camp about 3 o'clock we found it in a high state of excitement. During the morning the Ree scouts thrown out in advance had discovered the camp of a Sioux hunting party of 5 lodges. For some time they lay about it in the brush, watching the people at their various occupations, the women cutting up deer meat and drying it, and the children playing about. The men were absent, hunting. After the scouts had learned all that they could, they sent one of their number back and notified General Custer of their discovery. When he learned the facts, he hurried ahead and the first intimation the Indians had of the presence of white people in the Hills was when the General and a few officers rode into their camp. The Sioux, who were Ogalallas, were terrified.[38] The little ones bolted for the brush and the women wished to do the same, but had not time to escape. Through Louis Agard as interpreter, General Custer talked with the women and a few moments later with the men, when several of them came in. He offered the whole party of twenty-seven souls rations if they would travel with us until we got out of the Black Hills. This they refused to do. Then the General offered two of the men rations if they would go along with the command and guide it out of the Hills; but they refused this offer. Finally he asked them if they would stay and camp with us as long as we remained where we then were, and to this they agreed. It appeared that the wife of the head man, whose name was 'The One Who Stabs' or 'Stabber,' was a daughter of Red Cloud, and to be on good terms with any relation of Red Cloud's seemed very desirable.[39]

"The Sioux were then invited to come to our camp and receive some coffee and sugar and four of the six men came; The One Who Stabs, Slow Bull and two others. They were very suspicious, partly no doubt because of the presence among our scouts of a party of Rees, with whom the Sioux had long been at war. When they got to the camp, only two of them shook hands all around as is the custom. None of these Indians had at all the appearance of Agency Indians, and one of them looked especially wild and determined. He evidently had seen very few white men and was uneasy and uncomfortable. After the Sioux had sat about for a time and talked a little, and had received their food, they started back one by one toward their camp. The last ones to leave were the old chief, thé Stabber, and the wild fellow.

"These two had gone but a short distance when for some reason Lieutenant Wallace sent two of the Santee boys to call them back. When these boys overtook the Sioux, the four rode together for a few moments. The Santees delivered their message, and the wild fellow suddenly exclaimed, 'I may as well die to-day as tomorrow.' As he said this he seized the gun of the Santee who was riding by his side. The Santee was carrying the rifle before him on the saddle, and the Sioux caught it by the stock while Red Bird, the Santee, threw his weight on the barrel and at the same time jumped off his horse, thus retaining possession of the gun. He let go of his horse, however, and it ran away.

"When the Sioux lost the gun, he turned his horse — a beautiful cream pony — and lashed it up the hill toward the wood. Red Bird then began to shoot at him and fired four or five shots, wounding — as he believed — the pony.

"As soon as the shots were heard, the whole Ree outfit threw themselves on their horses and in five minutes were riding as hard as they could down the valley.

"The first impression in the camp had been that the Rees had attacked the Sioux village and were killing them all. This error was soon corrected by the appearance of Louis Agard and Cold Hand, one of our Sioux scouts, with two other scouts, who brought back with them the old chief. Then the true state of affairs was learned, and also the fact that the Sioux village had disappeared. No doubt while the men were getting their coffee and sugar at the camp, the women had hastily taken down the lodges, packed their horses and fled, to be overtaken later by the men. The Ree scouts followed the village for some time but did not overtake it. It was about ten o'clock before they returned to camp.

"Meantime General Custer with a few men and some scouts had started on the trail of the wild looking Indian, and followed it for some distance. Before going far, the Indian's saddle, with its blanket, his gun case, two more blankets and the sack of coffee that had been given him were found along the trail, all of them . . . bloody, as if the man or his horse had been wounded. Evidently as soon as he got out of sight of the boy who was shooting at him, the fleeing Indian cut loose everything his horse carried and then started on a long ride. This, of course, was quite in accordance with . . . Indian custom.

"That night when Captain North and I went over to the little fire by which Charley Reynolds and the two prospectors were seated, we talked . . . about the events of the day.

"'Why should that Indian have gotten rid of his saddle and his blankets?' said McKay. . . . 'He had far to go and would need a saddle; the nights are cold here in the hills and he would need blankets.'

"'True enough,' said Charley, 'but comfort and warmth don't count much when a man's life is in the balance. According to what that Santee boy said, this Indian was badly scared, and I don't doubt that he thought this whole outfit was going to take after him and try to capture him. He knew it was a big outfit, and likely one with lots of horses in it faster than his. He wanted to get away and he didn't mean that the horse should have a pound more to carry than was absolutely necessary, so he threw away everything that he had except his gun and . . . ammunition. If he was badly enough scared he would leave his horse after awhile somewhere in the brush or timber and would start on foot, because he knows a great deal better than most of us that it's nearly impossible to trail a man on foot. Isn't that so North?'

"'Yes,' said North, 'that is true enough. The Indians depend . . . on the swiftness of their horses, whether they're going into a fight or running away, and they understand . . . what a difference a few pounds of weight can make in what a horse can do, and how much freer a naked horse is than one that is cinched up with a stiff saddle on his back. When the Pawnees go into a fight they strip off everything from their horses and everything from themselves too. Sometimes when we'd be making a charge, it was funny to see them. They'd start perhaps with all their soldier clothes on and after making two or three miles, if I looked around, I'd see that they were all . . . stark naked and riding naked horses, just carrying their guns in their hands and . . . their cartridge boxes on their belts. On the other hand, if the enemy had been discovered, and we didn't have to make a quick charge they'd all stop, strip their horses and themselves, and throw saddles and clothing . . . down in a pile; maybe, if they had time, they'd paint themselves a little or tie a feather or a ribbon in their horse's forelock or tail, and then hop on naked and start into the fight. I guess it's that way with all Indians.'

" 'I'm a little surprised,' said Ross, 'that these Sioux didn't stop and camp with us. It's the first time I ever heard of an Indian's refusing free grub.'

" 'Well,' said North, 'I think they were plum scared to death. You see most of these Indians at Red Cloud [Agency] haven't seen very many white people; they've seen a few troops and had a lot of fights with them first and last, but probably they've never seen more than a hundred or a hundred and fifty white soldiers at one time.[40] Here comes along a big outfit four or five times larger than they've ever seen before, coming on them unexpectedly in a place where they had no idea of meeting anybody, and it frightens them nearly to death. Perhaps, too, some of them have taken part in fights or killings down south, and they know so little of white men's ways that they might easily enough think that this big body of troops was sent to capture them individually.'

" 'Yes,' said Charley, 'that's so too. I believe that we, none of us, know how simple these people are and how little they know about white men and the way white men think.'

" 'They saved the old man I hear,' said Ross.

" 'Yes,' said I, 'they have got him up at headquarters under guard, with a sentry in front of his tent and one at the back; and the General says . . . they are going to hold him until we get out of the Hills. Then I suppose they'll turn him loose, and he'll go back to his own people and be a great hero for all the rest of his days.'[41]

" 'Louis [Agard] says,' remarked Charley, 'that the old fellow is quite a big man down at the Agency and that old Red Cloud, his father-in-law, sets considerable store by him.'

" 'Wasn't it Red Cloud who was in command at the [Wm.] Fetterman killing?' I asked, directing my question to no one in particular.

" 'Yes,' said Charley, 'so I've always heard.'

" 'You ought to know Lute,' I said, 'you were down there nearer that country than any of the rest of us when it happened in '66.'

" 'Yes,' said North, 'Red Cloud was in command there, and he showed himself as good a soldier and strategist as the troops showed themselves ignorant of Indian ways.'

" 'Tell us the story Lute,' I said.

" 'Well,' he replied, 'I don't know that I can tell you the story very well. It's a pretty long one, and it has to do with the building of Fort Phil Kearney, right in the heart of the Sioux country, and after the Sioux, at a council held at Fort Laramie in the spring of 1866, had refused the permission asked by the Government to send troops through their country or to build a post there. This was the next year after my brother Frank had been north in the Powder River country with General [Patrick] Connor, where they had plenty of fighting with the Cheyenne and Arapaho. They had killed some Indians, but had never really whipped them, and for one or two days they had marched along within sight of a big party of Indians afraid to attack them, while the Indians thought the troops were too many for them to attack.

" 'Colonel [Henry B.] Carrington had been sent to build Fort Phil Kearney on the banks of Big Piny Creek not far from the Big-horn Mountains. The post was located on a little plateau, and after its limits had been marked out, Colonel Carrington began to send out parties to bring in logs to build the post. He had saw-mills, and the work of putting up the post with its partial stockade, bar-racks, storehouses, officers' quarters, and stables and corrals went on pretty fast. The garrison was a fairly large one, about six hun-dred men I believe, but they knew very well that all about them and watching them all the time were a great many hostile Indians who would try hard to cut off every straggler and small party . . . they could. The troops worked hard, and by fall the post was built, in the sense that the quarters were all under cover and the stockade completed.

" 'As the work went on the Indians seemed to grow bolder; twice they ran off a lot of horses that were feeding right close up to the stockade, and one time when a captain who was guarding a supply train allowed his men to unsaddle their horses and let them graze right close to the road, the Indians swooped down and drove off every hoof, and the escort walked the rest of the way. Along in . . . early winter a wood train was attacked only a couple of miles from the post, and sixty-five men in two parties under Colonel Carrington and Capt. Fetterman went out and drove them off, but the troops lost a lieutenant and a sergeant.

" 'A couple of weeks later another party went out to the timber, the train with its drivers and escort numbering about ninety men, all of them armed. Toward noon a lookout signalled that this outfit was surrounded and fighting, and eighty men were sent to help them out. Fetterman asked to be allowed to command it, and although it was not his turn to go out, as he was the senior officer present he was allowed to go. Captain Brown, the quartermaster, went with him as a volunteer, and another volunteer, a lieutenant, was given command of a small force of cavalry. Stopping at the post were two civilians who were traveling through the country, and they also volunteered. While these troops were getting ready to start, a number of Indians were seen on the hills round about, and two or three cannon shots were sent after them which scattered them and they disappeared. When Fetterman left the post, he started out to try to get around the Indians and cut them off, but before he had reached the foot-hills he met plenty of Indians and commenced to fight them, still advancing. It appeared afterwards that the Indians had left the wood train to go to meet Fetterman, and the train now started for the timber. Captain Fetterman and his command were seen from the post to go over the ridge and disappear. A few shots were heard. Then more and presently a steady shooting which showed that the troops and the Indians were fighting hard.

" 'A surgeon was sent out with instructions to go to Fetterman, but he could not get to him on account of the Indians. The train was all right, however. When Surgeon Hines found that he could not reach Captain Fetterman, he galloped back to the post and reported, and seventy-six more men were sent out, all of them mounted and rode straight to where the fighting was going on. By this time the shooting had grown less and only an occasional shot was heard, and at last even this stopped. There was a little snow on the ground, and when the relief party got to where Fetterman's command had crossed the ridge, they could see their tracks in the snow, but when they looked down in the valley they could see no soldiers, but plenty of Indians yelling and shouting apparently in triumph.

" 'The Captain who commanded the relief party saw that he was greatly outnumbered and hesitated to charge down the hill, but in a short time the Indians drew off and disappeared. Then the relief party went down into the Creek Valley and crossing it went up on a little ridge, and there in a very small space — not more than seventy-five or eighty feet square — lay the bodies of Captain Fetterman, Captain Brown and sixty-five men. They had been shot and lanced and pounded down with war clubs, and apparently it had been a pretty quick killing. One of the civilians was found lying close to a rock by the side of which was a little pile of Henry rifle cartridge shells, showing that he had done good work before he was killed.

" 'Lieutenant Grummond with a number of his men was found at a little distance from where the main portion of the command had been killed.'

" 'Then there were about eighty or ninety men killed in that fight?' I asked.

" 'Yes,' said Lute, 'nearer ninety than eighty. I never heard the exact number but as nearly as I could figure it, it was between eighty and ninety.'

" 'That was sure a big killing for the Indians,' said Charley, 'and it made their hearts plenty strong. They have been getting bolder ever since that time, and I expect they are looking forward to some other big victory like that when they will again conquer a good bunch of white men.' "[42] With tragic irony, Reynolds prophesied his own death, for two years later he would be one of the first to fall in the annihilation of Custer's forces at the Little Bighorn.

" 'Well,' I asked, 'was it ever definitely found out how many Indians there were in that [Fetterman] fight?'

" 'You can't prove it by me,' said Charley, 'I've heard all sorts of guesses, but I don't know anything about it.'

" 'Well,' said Lute,   'I heard from an officer at Fort Russell that there were more than two thousand Indians in the fight, most of them Sioux of course, but plenty of Cheyennes and Arapahos.'

" 'If Red Cloud was the general,' said Charley, 'as I've always supposed he was, he was a good soldier, but you'd think that anybody who was used to fighting Indians would not have allowed himself to be led into an ambush as those people were.'

" 'That's so,' said North, 'but the thing that always seemed queer to me was that those troops went out of the post and into action without carrying enough ammunition with them to make a fight. Everybody knows how soldiers waste ammunition, and here was a case where they knew that there were plenty of Indians, and they certainly ought to have carried a whole lot of cartridges with them.'

" 'Yes,' I said, 'we've all seen soldiers shoot, and we know that they can't shoot well. Of course, now and then there is a good shot, a man who knows his gun well, knows just how it's sighted, what trigger pull is and will take plenty of time, but most of them just fire in the general direction of anything they're trying to hit. I remember one time seeing a dozen antelope gallop by a company of soldiers, and the whole company just turned loose and kept shooting and they didn't touch a hair.'

" 'Besides that,' added North, 'those old Spencer carbines were a terror. You never could tell whether they were going to shoot straight ahead or round the corner.'

" 'I heard the General named this place where we are camped Castle Valley,' said Ross. 'That's not a . . . bad name, when you see the way in which these limestone ridges are weathered and worn into points.'

" 'No,' said Charley, 'this is a right pretty place and the hills here are a nice country. Lots of wood and water and grass.' "[43]

In concurring, Grinnell revealed an inchoate philosophy of preservation: " 'I don't wonder the Indians hate to have the white man come in, for of course if anybody should come in here and settle, the game would all be driven off pretty quick and like enough the hills burnt off too.' "[44]

As if to confirm these fears, Ross commented, " 'I reckon the white people are coming all right. Shall I show 'em that little bottle of mine, Charley?' he said, as he felt in his pocket.

" 'Of course,' said Charley.

" 'Well now, boys,' said Ross, addressing North and myself, 'don't say anything about this, but look here,' and he drew from his pocket a little vial which he passed over to me and which we both examined.

"It was full of small grains of yellow metal which we of course knew must be gold dust. Some of it was very fine, but occasionally there would be nuggets as large as the head of a pin and a few as large as half a grain of rice. We turned the bottle round and round and by the light of the fire looked at the shining yellow mass which did not much more than cover the bottom of the vial.

" 'That's gold I suppose,' said North, as he handed it back to the miner.

" 'Yes,' said Ross, 'that's gold, and found right on the surface, and where there is as much as that, there's bound to be lots more when we get down a little lower. I haven't shown this to anybody but Charley. If the boys knew we had got this, they'd throw away their rifles and begin to dig. Of course, I'll have to report it to the General, but he'll keep it quiet until we get out of the Hills. I shall go back with the command to Lincoln and then as quick as I can, I'll get an outfit and come back and winter here and locate some claims. There'll be lots of men in here this winter, I guess, but if not this winter, surely next spring.' "[45]

In such a seemingly insignificant way, the Black Hills gold rush of 1874–76 had its beginning. Custer, of course, did not keep the find a secret, and before long, the population centers to the east had the big news.

The night continued to serve up tragic prophecy. After Ross made his prediction about the coming influx of gold seekers, Grinnell commented sadly: " 'Well, that will mean an Indian war I expect, for the Sioux and Cheyennes won't give up this country without a fight.' "[46] Charley Reynolds agreed. He should have, for the Little Bighorn debacle was part of the Sioux war started by the discovery of the yellow metal.

" 'But the fight may not come right away,' " observed Reynolds.[47] " 'They'll try to get the Government to send troops to keep the miners out and to live up to the old treaties, but of course, the troops can't do anything if people think there's gold here.'

" 'Not a thing,' said Lute.

" 'Well,' I said, 'I hear we're going to lay over here tomorrow, but we had an early start this morning and I'm going to bed.'

" 'Yes,' said Ross, 'we'll lay over tomorrow and that means that Mac and I will be busy all day sinking prospect holes and shoveling dirt.'

" 'Well,' said North, 'if you were working for yourselves, I'd wish you good luck, but as it is, I rather believe that I hope you won't find anything. Goodnight,' and Lute and I went over to our tent in a headquarter line and were soon in bed and asleep."[48]

The next morning, Monday, July 27, "we slept late by comparison with other mornings; yet the sun was not high above the horizon when we were up and about. While we were eating breakfast, I saw Ross and McKay, leading a pack horse loaded with tools, start off down the stream, evidently looking for signs of precious metal. A little later two or three small scouting parties were sent out in various directions, and later still, Lute and I saddled up, and he with his rifle and I with my shot-gun, we started out to look for birds. We went through some open timber and pretty soon struck into a narrow valley, tributary to the stream on which we were camped, and we followed this up.

"By this time we were far away from any other members of the expedition, and the grass through which we rode was unmarked by the trail of man or animals. We both kept a good lookout for game but saw nothing. The grass in this valley grew lush, rank and high, almost up to the horses' bellies, and everywhere in it were beautiful wild flowers of many hues. In the little willows that grew along the streams were many common birds, cat-birds, towhees and song sparrows, as well as other sparrows that were not recognized, and at the approach of the horses they dived down into the grass or bushes and were not seen again.

"At last turning into the timber, we rode for a little while in the cool green shade. Here a brood of ruffed grouse was startled, the little ones hardly more than half the size of quail, yet active and quick of wing and flying up into the branches of the trees where they stood motionless with outstretched necks. The mother meantime walked uneasily about and gradually increased her distance from us, perhaps in the hope that we would follow her. She did not resort to the device so frequently employed by ruffed grouse when the young are too small to fly, that of pretending to be wounded until she has drawn the enemy away from the place where her young are hidden.

"Arctic [mountain] bluebirds were abundant along the edges of the little valley and in the timber, and high up among the branches of the tall pines were seen a number of the beautiful western tanager. Some of these were so high above the ground that I seemed unable to reach them with the light loads in my gun, but I secured two or three specimens, one being a male in full plumage, and another a young male, whose throat and chin showed only traces of the crimson so noticeable in the adult male bird.

"By a beautiful cold spring which gushed out of a hillside from beneath a great rock, Lute and I sat down to smoke. We were delighted with the beauty and the freshness of the hills, so charming by contrast with the arid plains that we had passed over between the Missouri River and the Belle Fourche.

"'Yes,' said Lute, in response to some remark of mine, 'this is certainly a mighty pretty country. There must be plenty of rain here. Look at the way the grass grows and the flowers. Of course, I don't know whether crops would grow, but I don't see why they might not. I don't think the altitude is very great.'

"'No,' said I, 'I don't think it is. At the same time it's a great deal cooler here than it is down on the prairie, and I suspect that you'll find that spring comes here late and autumn comes early. I doubt if corn would ripen here.'

"'No,' said Lute, 'I guess likely corn would not ripen, but there might be lots of other crops that would.'

"'Perhaps so,' I responded, 'but after all it doesn't strike me as an agricultural country. In the first place there isn't arable land enough to make it pay to farm; nothing but these little narrow valleys. I should suppose that the greatest crop here would be the timber, and if you were to dam up most any one of those little valleys, you'd get water power enough to run saw-mills.'

"'That's so,' said Lute, 'but I guess there's lots of timber left that's a good deal closer to a market than this is.'

"'Of course, that is true,' I acknowledged, 'but I was thinking of a time when settlers come in here. Of course, if what Ross showed us last night is genuine, there's likely to be quite a rush for the Hills next summer, and the settlers and miners will want lumber for their houses and for many other purposes.'

" 'Well,' said Lute, 'this place is good enough for me as it is. I should hate mightily to see it full of people.'

" 'So should I.'

" 'We each of us rolled and smoked a last cigarette and then climbing on our horses again, we went on our way. It was late in the afternoon when . . . we came into camp. . . . For the rest of the afternoon I was busy skinning birds, and we were visited by a number of the Ree scouts who seemed to enjoy sitting and watching me at my work, while they gossiped about various happenings of the trip. . . .

"During the afternoon our friend, Wood, the civilian assistant of Captain Ludlow, came in and gave me a female ruffed grouse, which he had come across during the day and killed with his pistol. He told me that she had had a brood of half-grown young with her when he killed her. I skinned the specimen.

"That night seated about the headquarters' campfire I listened to General Custer and some of his officers recalling various incidents of the fighting which took place down in the Indian territory in 1868 between the troops and the Cheyennes and Arapahos. I did not know the history of that fight but had heard of the destruction of a Cheyenne village down there, and of the killing of Black Kettle, and it was interesting to hear these men talk about this fight."[49] In the years ahead Grinnell would sit around other campfires and hear a different version of the red-white struggle — this time from the Indians.

After several more days of travel, they reached the southern end of the Black Hills. On the morning of August 2, Custer "sent two companies of cavalry under Colonel [Verling K.] Hart south toward the Cheyenne River [south fork] to get an idea of the country lying between the Hills and that stream. Thinking that badlands containing fossils might be found near the River, Capt. North and I accompanied it. The ride, which took two or three days, was hard and rough. We had no guide, and for some reason or other struck most of the ravines and water courses at right angles, climbing down one very steep side and then up the other.[50]

Before we had reached the River, the provisions of the outfit were exhausted, and the horses, already weak and worn-out, began to fail. A number of them were killed, and their saddles and equipment burned. The men took from their saddle pockets their rations — a little bacon and hard bread — put the food in their shirts and walked after the command. Curiously enough our horses lasted, partly perhaps because we had saved them as much as we could. We got back to the command on the third or fourth day, extraordinarily hungry and bringing with us no fossils except a part of the lower jaw of a rhinoceros."[51]

Before Grinnell had left on the second to look for fossils, he heard that Charley Reynolds was going to leave the expedition to take Custer's dispatches into Fort Laramie. "Lute North and I were very anxious to make the ride with him. He professed himself willing to have our company, but there was, of course, no reason why we should go. Our horses were unfit to make the ride, and three men would have been much more likely to be detected by Indians than one going alone. Reynolds therefore started off by himself, riding a dapple brown horse procured from one of the wagon masters, a splendid-looking horse, but one that seemed vicious. Charley made the ride chiefly at night, hiding during the day. He got through without trouble, except that he suffered one day for lack of water. On a number of occasions he saw passing Indians from his place of concealment."[52]

Not long after Reynolds was sent out with the news of the gold discovery, the expedition began its return journey to Fort Lincoln. "One day just before leaving the Hills, Captain North, when three or four miles off to one side of the command, saw no less than five bears traveling along together on the prairie half a mile distant. If he had had a horse that could run, he might have attempted to kill some of them. About this time the Sioux, Cold Hand, and a young Ree came on an old grizzly bear and two yearling cubs, which they attacked. The bears ran out toward the prairie, and the Indians followed on horseback. They killed first one cub and then the other, but the mother kept far ahead of them. Finally their horses gave out and could carry them no further. Cold Hand, a cripple, could not go on, but the young Ree kept after the old bear on foot and finally killed her in a water hole where she had taken refuge. These skins and the skulls which went with them were purchased by Prof. Winchell and are believed now to be among the collections of the University of Minnesota."[53]

The whites also killed a number of grizzlies. Once, while Grinnell and North were placidly sitting behind a hill enjoying the scenery and eating wild raspberries, they heard what sounded like a "bombardment" nearby. Running to investigate the source of the commotion, they discovered Custer, Ludlow, and Bloody Knife standing over an old male bear with numerous bullet holes in its carcass. An argument was going on as to who was the rightful owner of the trophy. "The bear was dead before we reached the spot," North later commented, "so I didn't have a chance to get in a shot and claim that I killed it."[54]

Custer, of course, finally got the credit, and that night he proudly sent portions of meat to the different messes. His largess was not appreciated, however, "for it was tough and very strong. Bear meat from a young animal is good, but from an old one is hardly fit to eat."[55]

On the return journey, Custer, as usual, spent much of his time bragging about his ability as a hunter and marksman. He had with him some greyhounds that he claimed had caught antelope on the run. Even though the dogs frequently chased these swift animals, they never caught any, but they did manage to run down some jack rabbits.[56]

"Custer did no shooting that was notable. It was observed that, though he enjoyed telling of the remarkable shots that he himself commonly made, he did not seem greatly interested in the shooting done by other people. On one occasion when . . . North and I were traveling not far from the command, three deer frightened by its passage ran by us and North killed the three with three successive shots. That day when we reached camp, I took the saddle of one of the deer over to the general's tent and when I gave it to him, said, 'Captain North did some remarkable shooting today. He killed three running deer in three shots.' Custer's response to this remark was, 'Huh, I found two more horned toads today.'

"As we were returning to Fort Lincoln and were crossing the Bad Lands of the Missouri, while riding with . . . Custer ahead of the command we came to a small pond, near which a duck had nested. Seven or eight half grown young ones were swimming about and . . . Custer got off his horse and said, 'I will knock the heads off a few of them.'

"I looked at Luther North and made a sign to him and he dismounted and sat down on the ground behind the general. . . . Custer fired at a bird and missed it and North shot and cut the head off one of the birds. Custer shot again and missed and North cut the head off another bird. Custer looked around at him and then shot again and again missed and North cut the head off a third duck.

"Just then an officer rode up over a hill near the pond and said that the bullets after skipping off the water were singing over the heads of his troops. The general said, 'We had better stop shooting'; and mounted the horse and rode on without saying a word."[57]

On the return trip many of the men were concerned that part or all of the expedition might be attacked by hostile Indians. "From time to time we saw signal smokes not far off, indicating, as we then supposed, that wild Indians were exchanging signals about us. In mid-August some of the Indian scouts, while at a distance from the command, met a traveling party of agency Indians, who informed them that on the Little Missouri River there were six bands of hostile Indians waiting for our return and that when we reached there they purposed to fight us."[58]

"Soon after crossing the Little Missouri . . . , the abandoned camp was found of a great body of Indians."[59] This was probably the stopping place of the same aborigines spoken of by the friendly Indians. "In conversation that evening in front of General Custer's tent, . . . North remarked that perhaps it was just as well the Indians had gone before the expedition got there, as there were a great many of them. Custer commented, 'I could whip all the Indians in the northwest with the Seventh Cavalry.' "[60]

At 4:30 P.M., on August 30, 1874, the command arrived before the gates of Fort Lincoln, having taken sixty days to traverse 883 miles.[61] The accomplishments of the reconnaissance were mixed. Though valuable scientific reports had been compiled and 1,205 miles surveyed, the discovery of gold led to an Indian war and much bloodshed.

Despite his complaint that "the rapidity with which the command traveled admitted of but a very hasty and incomplete survey of the region," Grinnell did succeed in obtaining a significant collection of fossils, including some new to science.[62] Besides the report on paleontology, made as Marsh's representative, Grinnell also wrote one at Ludlow's request on the birds and mammals of the region traversed. For many years this monograph remained the definitive work on the Black Hills and vicinity. The section on mammals is particularly interesting, since some of the subspecies described are now extinct.[63] The larger forms most commonly observed were antelope, deer, and wolves. In regard to the latter Grinnell noted: "I found the gray wolf one of the most common animals in the Black Hills, and hardly a day passed without my seeing several individuals of this species. . . . Their howlings were often heard at night; and on one occasion I heard that doleful sound at midday — a bad omen, if we may trust the Indians."[64]

A few bighorn sheep, grizzly bears, and elk were also seen, but no buffalo.[65] Although elk were not often actually sighted, their presence was everywhere evident in the form of shed antlers. On one occasion a giant stack of these was found, inspiring the name "Elkhorn Prairie." For some unknown reason, they had been piled up by the Sioux.[66]

After putting the finishing touches on his report, Grinnell joined Captain Ludlow at the railhead, and together they boarded an eastbound train. "Ludlow and his outfit returned to St. Paul, and I went back to New York and New Haven."[67]

5

Inspecting
The "National Park"

WITH RELUCTANCE, Grinnell shed the role of explorer and resumed the more commonplace life of the graduate student. But as a member of Yale's Sheffield Scientific School and an assistant to Marsh in the Peabody Museum, he had little time for regretting his mundane existence. [1] Even his weekends were spent feverishly collecting birds at his father's farm in Milford, Connecticut. The notes taken on these specimens were given to the future chief of the Biological Survey, C. Hart Merriam, and became the basis of his important work, *A Review of the Birds of Connecticut* (1877). [2]

Sooner than he thought possible, Grinnell had another chance to play explorer. The reports he had compiled on the paleontology and zoology of the Black Hills region and his general performance during the expedition had favorably impressed Captain Ludlow. "In the spring of 1875 ... Ludlow wrote me saying that in the summer he expected to be ordered to make a reconnaissance in Montana and asked me to go with him as naturalist. He could pay me nothing, nor even furnish railroad transportation, but he would

[108]

subsist me in the field and furnish me what was needed there. Prof. Marsh seemed to think it desirable that I go."[3]

The purpose of the reconnaissance was to survey Yellowstone National Park. White men had been passing through the area, though not necessarily in the Park proper, since at least the time of John Colter, a hunter for Lewis and Clark. A later visitor was that ubiquitous mountain man, Jim Bridger, who stumbled across the wondrous land of geysers, waterfalls, and hot springs in 1830. Although he told the outside world of his find, everyone "knew" that mountain men were notorious storytellers, and "Old Jim Bridger's lies" were long a source of amusement.[4] Not until forty years later did the real "discovery" of the region occur, "by which is meant its full and final disclosure to the world."[5] After the return of two expeditions made in 1869 and 1870, Bridger was no longer ridiculed.

In 1872 Congress set the region aside as the nation's first national park, but with the idea that the area was a "museum" of "curiosities" or "wonders" and not a national park in anything like the present conception of the term.[6] Because the Park's boundaries were drawn with little real knowledge of the terrain, a number of expeditions were sent into the region to see exactly what Congress had, in fact, preserved.[7] The Ludlow reconnaissance of 1875 was one of these.

Before heading west, Grinnell arranged to have his close friend and Yale classmate, Edward Salisbury Dana, accompany him. Then a tutor at the college, Dana was the son of James Dwight Dana, a Yale professor since 1850 and the country's leading geological expert. The younger Dana "had never been in the West, and this seemed to me a good opportunity for him to see something of the untouched Western country. I therefore wrote Ludlow asking if he did not wish to have Dana, provided the latter could get away, and saying that Dana was competent to report on the geology of the country passed over. Capt. Ludlow at once accepted the suggestion, and when I broached the matter to Dana, he was glad to go.

"We left New Haven about the middle of June, joined Ludlow and Wood, and Ludlow's brother Ned, at St. Paul, and then went west to Bismarck, which we reached July 2nd. The 7th Cavalry was not expected to be ordered out that summer, for Gen. Custer was very unjustly under suspicion of being concerned with the sale of certain post traderships, and was more or less under a cloud at Washington. Ludlow succeeded in having Charley Reynolds detailed to go with him, and also Lieut. R. E. Thompson — Dick Thompson — an infantry officer."[8]

The party stayed in Bismarck several days and then boarded the steamer *Josephine*, bound for the outpost of Carroll on the margin of the Judith Basin in Montana Territory. On the way, the expedition was expected to stop at forts Stevenson, Berthold, Buford, and Peck. At Carroll, the group was to pick up a cavalry escort from Fort Ellis, located near the present town of Bozeman, and then travel south to the Park.[9]

"On the way up the river . . . Ned Ludlow was taken sick, and his brother felt it necessary to stop over at Ft. Buford to see the post surgeon there. The rest of the party went on, and Capt. Ludlow and his brother were to follow on the next boat. Meantime the command devolved on Lieut. Thompson."[10]

In 1875 the upper Missouri was still a wilderness in almost pristine condition. An illustration of this fact is that the grizzly bear, animal of the deepest wilds, continued to live along the river's banks. As Grinnell and Reynolds were conversing on the steamer's deck the evening of July 10, the same day the party left Fort Buford, Grinnell happened to spot a grizzly in a wide open bottom on the south side of the river, not far below the mouth of Poplar River. When he pointed out the animal, Reynolds looked in that direction and was able to locate two more bears back in the undergrowth and farther off than the first.[11]

"When we reached Carroll, we found it to consist of two trading stores and about a dozen log cabins. Our cavalry escort was waiting for us, under command of Lieut. Chas. F. Roe, 2nd Cavalry, who subsequently attained fame as the Commander in Chief of the National Guard of the State of New York.

"Carroll — named for Mat Carroll, a trader at Ft. Benton in the '60's — was on the border of the Judith Basin, which was then a sort of debatable ground roamed over by half a dozen tribes of Indians, all at war among themselves and most of them with the whites. We learned that the Indians were then rather bad and that a night or two before we reached Carroll, they had entered the town and taken from it every horse there except one crippled animal that was unable to walk. They had also taken all the horses from the stage and freight stations along the road, and while they had not killed any people, that was thought to be chiefly because they had not had an opportunity to do so.

"Lieut. Roe, of course, had brought in our transportation, and we did not suffer from the raid of the Indians. We moved out a few miles from Carroll and went into camp on Crooked Creek, waiting for the boat which would bring Capt. Ludlow. There were buffalo in the country, and plenty of antelope, and in the mountains not far off there were deer, sheep and some elk."[12]

Pronghorn seemed to be the most abundant large animal, but buffalo still roamed the area in huge numbers. Grinnell saw "places in a peculiarly fine, powdery soil . . . where . . . [bison] trails were . . . two feet deep. The buffalo passed over them in single file, backward and forward, many animals daily. . . . In places where they followed down through . . . ravines, from the high prairie to the level of the river bottom, they became extra deep."[13]

"We did a little hunting, and Dana and I did some geologizing."[14] Actually, the two did more than just "some" geology work. As one of the expedition's soldiers noted in his diary, "Scientific parties make their daily explorations after fossils, etc. Professor Grinnell and Mr. Dana are constantly in the saddle, busy providing matter for their respective reports."[15]

"As usual on such expeditions" — Grinnell complained — "we were mounted on condemned army horses which were perfectly able to carry us about over the prairie at a walk, but could not do much running. On one of these days, while waiting for Capt. Ludlow, I was perhaps more frightened than I have ever been before or since. When I had parted from Mrs. Dana, Ned's mother, just as we were leaving New Haven, she had said to me as we shook hands, 'Good bye, Mr. Grinnell; take good care of my boy.' I had been out West three or four seasons, and knew a little about the ways of the country. Dana had never been in the West and was as ignorant of its dangers as it was possible . . . to be. I felt, therefore, that I must constantly look after him, to see that he did not . . . get into . . . trouble.

"On the day of my fright, Dana and I were eight or ten miles from camp. We were examining an outcrop of rock on a knoll, and he had dismounted to investigate it with his geological hammer. While he was pounding away, I sat on my horse looking over the prairie, for I was prepared at any moment to see some of the Indians of whom we had heard so much. Presently half a dozen men rode up out of a hollow a mile or more away and galloped toward us.

"I knew of no whites in the country and felt that these men were probably Indians, and I called to Dana to get on his horse. It was useless to run, for almost anything that went on four legs would have overtaken our horses, and the approaching riders, though still far off, were coming toward us rapidly. There seemed but one thing to do and that was to prepare to fight — at all events to keep them at a distance. Dana would not be very helpful in a battle, not because he did not wish to help, but because he did not know how."[16] Remembering the example of Lute North when the Cheyennes attacked three summers before, Grinnell told Dana "to dismount and stand behind his horse and to do what he saw me do. I dismounted, and when the riders were 400 or 500 yards off, I pointed my gun at them. Meantime I had noticed that the leading man of the party seemed to be wearing a blanket and a pair of red leggings.

"When these people saw us dismount, they stopped and one of them, riding out to one side, took off his hat and swung it in the air. They had been so distant that up to this time, I had not seen that any one of them wore a hat. This seemed good evidence that they were white men, since the Indians of those days did not wear hats. We allowed them to come up, and they proved to be a little party led by a well-known character of the day called 'Liver Eating Johnson.' The man in the blanket and red leggings was a negro, dressed in a heavy overcoat and a pair of red drawers. The men with them were an Indian and a half-breed and two white men.

"Johnson announced he had left a sick man in camp and was looking about to find someone who had some liquor for him. Of course we had none. As a matter of fact, I presume that Johnson, who was notoriously a practical joker, had ridden toward us with the idea that we might be stampeded and perhaps chased into our camp, which he would greatly have enjoyed. I afterward learned that Johnson and the negro had been camped for some weeks with the Crows.... If these had been Indians, as I had feared, they might perhaps have killed both Dana and myself, though, to be sure, few Indians of that day had good guns. Most of them still carried bows and arrows, and those who possessed firearms had muzzle loaders, whose accurate range was only about 100 yards."[17] Proudly Grinnell recalled that "when we reached camp and told our story, Dana and I received high commendation from Charley Reynolds for our discretion in not permitting the strangers to come near until we learned something about them.

"We stayed two or three days more on Crooked Creek, and then as our supplies were running low, we started on . . . to Camp Lewis on the Big Spring Fork of the Judith River, near where Lewistown, Montana, now stands. Then there was a military camp, under the command of a captain of infantry, and a small log trading post which belonged to Reed and Bowles.

"These two men were . . . extraordinary characters. Reed had come into Montana from Colorado in 1868 and had become an Indian agent for the Gros Ventre and Assiniboine Indians. He was popular with the . . . Indians, and after losing his position as . . . agent, about 1871 or 1872, he established the trading post with Bowles.

"Reed and Bowles were men of the greatest courage. It used to be told that on one occasion at a gathering of Indians, one of them without provocation shot Reed's dog, whereupon Reed promptly killed the Indian. This act, while resented, was regarded more or less as a private quarrel, and Reed was not attacked. He afterward settled the matter by giving certain presents of horses and trade goods to the Indian's relatives.

"Bowles had married a Piegan woman, who of course was with him at the post on Big Spring Fork.[18] Early in 1878, a small party of Piegans, some of them relatives of Bowles' wife, who were out on a hunting and horse stealing trip, stopped at the trading store and that night disappeared, and with them Bowles' wife. Suspecting what had happened, Bowles mounted a good horse and followed the party, overtaking them the next morning just as they were about to move camp. In the ensuing dispute Bowles killed two of the men, while the other ran away. He brought his wife back with him to the trading post, where she remained.

"Reed died in Seattle, Washington, in the summer of 1912. Bowles, I think, was killed in Montana long before that."[19]

The expedition's "ride into Camp Lewis had been long, dry and dusty, and the sight of the beautiful, clear stream was very attractive. When we reached the camp, the captain in command told us some of his troubles. A number of his men were raw recruits, wholly new to the plains. The evening before, three of them had gone out fishing in the stream, and while thus engaged, sixteen Sioux Indians had swept down out of a ravine, killed the three men, driven off the horses and mules belonging to the camp, and disappeared into the hills.

"A mile and a half below Camp Lewis, there was a great village — 300 lodges — of Crow Indians, bitter enemies of the Sioux.[20] Word was sent to them, and a lot of the Indians came up to the soldier camp."[21] After a short conference, "the Crows rushed back to their camp, got together some warriors and set out in pursuit of the Sioux. . . . Before the sun had set, a force of 100 Crows had started on the trail of the Sioux, and nothing had been heard of them since they left."[22] In the meantime the Crow women and children moved close to the whites for safety.

"As I say, we were hot, tired and dusty, and I proposed to Charley Reynolds that while supper was being cooked, we should go down to the stream and take a swim. He agreed and we started. The best and deepest pool seemed to be the one about which were the graves of the three recruits killed the night before, for the soldiers had buried them just where they had fallen.

"Reynolds and I were soon undressed, and leaving our arms with our clothes, we were ducking and splashing in the water like a couple of ducks that had not seen the element for months. Suddenly we were startled by a shot which sounded from the bank immediately over us. We swam to shore, got our rifles and cartridge belts, and clad only in these crept to the edge of the bank, and raised our heads to look through the grass and sagebrush. Only a short distance from the stream and riding briskly down the valley, we saw three Indians, the one in the middle naked and carrying a pole, from the top of which waved a scalp, the other two clad in elaborate war costumes and singing in triumph, while from time to time they fired their guns. Evidently these were messengers from the returning successful Crow war party.

"Our fears set at rest, Charley and I dressed as rapidly as possible and came out on the bank. Looking down the valley, we could see from the Crow camp a procession of old men, women and children coming up the valley; while from the other direction, slowly coming down the valley, a number of Crow warriors were constantly appearing over the hill, all singing triumph songs and shooting off their guns. As they drew near, we could see loose horses captured from the Sioux driven along by little groups, or a man, as he rode by singing in triumph, hold up a captured gun, or bow case and quiver, or a shield. When the advancing warriors met them, the people from the camp drew off on either side, and the men passed down a lane, while the women and children and old men joined their songs and cries of triumph to those of the warriors."[23]

Triumph was not the only emotion in the Crow camp that evening; sorrow, too, was there. "After the fighting contingent had passed, there was seen coming over the crest of the hill on foot a shock-headed Indian boy, who led a mule bearing a bundle done up in a green blanket. Following the mule were an elderly man, a woman and a young man, all wailing in sorrow. The mule bore, as we learned afterward, the body of Long Horse, the chief, the only man lost by the Crows.

"The Crows had followed the Sioux until well after dark, when they had hidden themselves in the mountains to see what might happen. The Sioux, after running for a time and finding that they had not been overtaken, had apparently determined to return to the soldier camp and perhaps kill more people and take more horses. On their return they followed their trail back again. The Crows let them come on until they had passed well within the ambuscade and then had risen up and killed 7 of the 16. Long Horse, rushing up to count coup on a fallen man, had been shot and killed by a dying Sioux.[24]

"After the mourning party had passed us, Reynolds and I followed them down toward the camp."[25] Walking behind the Crow funeral procession in mute fascination, Grinnell was amazed at what he saw next. "When they reached the sutler's store the old woman dismounted from her horse, and walking over to a wagon that stood by the building, she drew her butcher knife, placed her little finger on the wagon wheel, and by a quick stroke cut off the finger. She then gashed the top of her head three or four times with the point of the knife, so that the blood streamed down over her face. 'There,' said Charley to me, 'you see that those people are really sorry for their loss.' "[26]

This ritual mutilation, so necessary to the correct, public display of mourning, was not over yet. "Later in the day Long Horse's brother came into the store, and walking over to the end of the counter where there stood under a screen a large cheese with a knife for cutting it, he opened the screen, took out the knife, and rested his little finger on the counter and cut it off. It was said that Long Horse was buried in a lodge not far from the Crow camp, reclining on his bed covered with robes, his face handsomely painted.

"The next day our party went on."[27] It was probably when the expedition was pulling out, as Grinnell and Reynolds were stopping off at the trading post for some last-minute items, that the young Easterner ran into Luther S. ("Yellowstone") Kelly, the well-known explorer and scout. "But it was only for a moment," remembered Kelly, "and he was off with his guide. In that lonely region, teeming with game and . . . flora, he had no time to spare."[28]

Heading ever south, the party struck the Musselshell River on August 4, and "two days later we reached Camp Baker, Montana, a military post, where Major H. B. Freeman of infantry was in command. Major and Mrs. Freeman were extremely kind to us, and we could do nothing but accept their hospitality. Major Freeman, who was a great angler, took us over to Camas Creek, where we had a chance to land some big grayling. We stayed at Camp Baker for two or three days. There was here an interesting exposure of Potsdam sandstone, from which we extracted many trilobites. Later I was able to kill a nice, fat antelope, which I sent back to Mrs. Freeman.

"We left Camp Baker August 7th and reached Ft. Ellis the

evening of the 9th. . . . I do not recall the commanding officer
at Ellis at this time, but . . . the young lieutenants were . . . extremely kind and hospitable and made our stay at Ellis very
delightful.

"From Ellis we rode over . . . to Bottler's ranch on the Yellowstone, where we camped. In the [surrounding] . . . mountains
were plenty of bears, deer and sheep. We killed some elk. Near
Bottler's we saw young buffalo feeding with the cattle."[29]

The expedition finally reached the Park area the middle of
August. As the column traveled through the Yellowstone region,
it continually encountered skin hunters. The completion of the
transcontinental railroad to the south had made this great game
country readily accessible, along with the Eastern tanneries that
called for the hides of all larger mammals. A railroad system
and more modern weapons enabled the hide hunters to kill game
in the systematic fashion demanded by the processing factories.

When the 1869 and 1870 Yellowstone expeditions confirmed
the rumors of tremendous game concentrations, the stage was set
for an influx of skin hunters. By the time the Ludlow party
entered the area, they were there in force. This new slaughter
would make the killing Audubon had witnessed a generation
before seem trifling by comparison. In a sense it was part of
another "rediscovery of the West," in terms of a more systematic,
commercial exploitation of the region's natural resources, particularly the most readily utilized resource, its fantastically
abundant wildlife.

Grinnell and Ludlow both experienced anguish at finding the
destroyers in the heart of the nation's only national park. Because
Ludlow was an outspoken critic of those who would mistreat
the Indians and despoil the environment, Grinnell "had a very
great admiration" for the Captain.[30] In the face of Custer's demand on the 1874 expedition that the government break the
treaty with the Sioux and open the Black Hills to whites, Ludlow
had asked that the area remain in the hands of the Dakotas.[31]
Now, once again, he took a firm stand. The issue this time was
Washington's neglect of the national park, which allowed the free
rein not only of skin hunters but timber thieves and souvenir
collectors as well. (The latter were cutting up geyserite and

carting it off by the wagon load.) Ludlow knew that if the government would only assume its obligation, "The day will come . . . when this most interesting region, crowded with marvels and adorned with the most superb scenery, will be rendered accessible to all; then, thronged with visitors from all over the world, it will be what nature and Congress, for once working together in unison, have declared it should be, a National Park."[32]

Grinnell now had everything he needed to make an attack on the hated hide hunters. His official standing as the Ludlow expedition's naturalist gave him a vehicle for articulating his viewpoint, and the sympathy of his superior assured that his opinion would receive a friendly welcome. Preceding his zoological report, published by the government as part of the papers of the reconnaissance, Grinnell included a "Letter of Transmittal," dated June 1, 1876, and addressed to Ludlow. It read: "It may not be out of place here to call . . . attention to the terrible destruction of large game, for the hides alone, which is constantly going on in those portions of Montana and Wyoming through which we passed. Buffalo, elk, mule deer and antelope are being slaughtered by thousands each year, without regard to age or sex, and at all seasons. Of the vast majority of animals killed, the hide only is taken. Females of all these species are as eagerly pursued in the spring, when just about to bring forth their young, as at any other time.

"It is estimated that during the winter of 1874–75 not less than 3,000 elk were killed for their hides alone . . . . Buffalo and mule deer suffer even more severely than the elk, and antelope nearly as much. The Territories referred to have game laws, but, of course, they are imperfect and cannot, in the present condition of the country, be enforced. Much, however, might be done to prevent the reckless destruction of the animals to which I have referred by the officers stationed on the frontier, and a little exertion in this direction would be well repaid by the increase of large game in the vicinity of the posts where it was not unnecessarily and wantonly destroyed . . . . The general feeling of the better class of frontiersmen, guides, hunters, and settlers is strongly against those who are engaged in this work of butchery, and all, I think, would be glad to have this wholesale

Charley Reynolds.

Edward Salisbury Dana.

Old Peabody Museum.

Grizzly bear killed by Custer and his companions. From left to right, the men in the photograph are Bloody Knife, Custer, Custer's orderly and Captain William Ludlow.

Cheyenne, Wyoming, as it looked about 1884, when Grinnell used to stop there on business while en route to his ranch.

Fort Abraham Lincoln, Dakota Territory. (The photograph is from a broken plate.)

Aerial photograph of the Como "Bluffs" in Wyoming, the famous "dinosaur field" in which Grinnell worked.

Custer's wagon train pulled up into four columns on the prairie, near the present state line between North and South Dakota.

A rest stop on the Custer expedition. (The photograph is from a broken plate.)

One of Custer's camps in the Black Hills.

Fort Clagett, Montana Territory.

The *Josephine,* the stern-wheeler Grinnell and his companions took up the Missouri

Judge Carter's home at Fort Bridger.

Fort Ellis, Montana Territory.

Enlarged section showing Winchell, North, and Grinnell standing together.

Men of the Black Hills expedition. Ludlow, leader of the 1875 Yellowstone reconnaissance, is sitting on the far left; standing behind and to the right of him is McIntosh; the three men standing together to the left of the tent are, from left to right, Winchell, North, and Grinnell; sitting to the right of Grinnell is Forsyth; Bloody Knife (with long hair) is standing in front of the tent's door; and Custer is lying down in the middle.

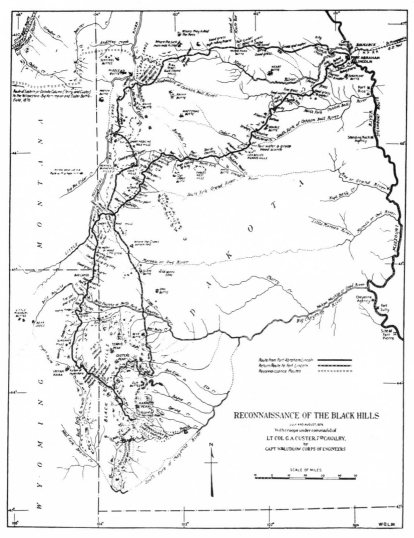

Ludlow's map showing Custer's route to and from the Black Hills.

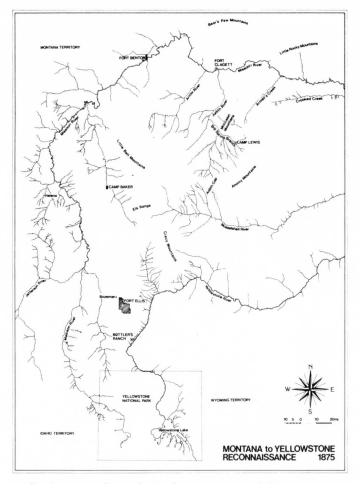

Ludlow's map, redrawn by Andrea Brewster, of the country traversed on the Yellowstone National Park expedition.

Plum Creek Station (now Lexington), Nebraska, as it looked in 1872 when Grinnell and his companions left there to meet the Pawnees and accompany them on their summer buffalo hunt.

UNION PACIFIC RAILROAD PHOTO

Custer's wagon train passing through the Black Hills.

William Frederick ("Buffalo Bill") Cody.

Reed and Bowles trading post with unindentified persons. (The photograph was taken in 1925.

The officers' quarters of Fort Bridger, circa 1870. The civilian third from the left is probably Judge William A. Carter.

The Santa Barbara Mission circa 1875, one of the "sights" Grinnell visited on his trip to Southern California.

San Francisco as it looked shortly before Grinnell's visit in 1881.

Hunters in North Park, Colorado, circa 1880.

Grinnell in Montana in his later years.

and short-sighted slaughter put a stop to. But it is needless to enlarge upon this abuse. The facts concerning it are well known to most Army officers and to all inhabitants. . . . It is certain that, unless in some way the destruction of these animals can be checked, the large game still so abundant in some localities will ere long be exterminated."[33]

Grinnell had no objection to hunting big game for food or a trophy — he was an avid hunter himself — but he despised those who destroyed game by the wagon load, without regard to sex or season. He realized that those who hunted for sport were no threat to wildlife. Instead, it was the commercialization of game, which encouraged its systematic destruction, that threatened so many species with extinction. His letter was one of the first official protests of its kind. From the more sophisticated, academic approaches to Western exploration, represented by paleontology and zoology, a new concern for the natural world was evolving which would finally culminate in the conservation movement.

After leaving Yellowstone Park and heading north to the Missouri, Grinnell and his companions "heard from a party of skin hunters that Indians were still in the country. At a camp near the Moccasin Mountains, perhaps on Armell's Creek, the sentry one morning just before dawn fired a shot which brought the whole outfit out of its blankets. Capt. Ludlow and the Sergeant were shouting to the men to secure their horses, while the others of us, having put on our shoes — and nothing else — with cartridge belt in one hand and rifle in the other, were hurrying out toward the crest of the hill behind which the sentry stood. The soldier could tell little about what he had shot at. He had seen something moving and challenged it, and when it did not answer, fired. As the faint light grew stronger and stronger, we stood there peering off over the prairie intently waiting, watching. Presently someone saw something moving, and a few moments later this something was seen to be a great skunk that was playing around on the hillside. Our disgust may be imagined.

"At about this point the outfit separated. Ludlow and Dana went on to Carroll, crossed the river and made an excursion into the Little Rocky Mountains, where Dana killed a buffalo and an antelope. Reynolds, Wood and I went down into the valley of the Judith, where I examined washed bluffs and found a few dinosaur remains and a good many invertebrate fossils. Reed [of the trading post] went with us to point out the way for the wagon, and we found a camp of Gros Ventre Indians at the mouth of the river, outside Ft. Clagett.

"We had been in the valley of the Judith only two or three days when a messenger from Carroll arrived, ordering us back there to catch the last boat that would run on the river. Wood, with the wagons and the outfit, started back overland, while Reynolds, Ned Ludlow, and I, finding a Mackinaw boat at Clagett's, bought it, loaded our beds into it, and started down the Missouri. We left the mouth of the Judith at 3:13, September 16th."[34]

"In those days this was a game country. There were plenty of buffalo, besides smaller game. . . . "[35] "On the way down the river we killed two mule deer, an elk and a mountain sheep, and by that time had the boat so loaded that it would hold nothing more."[36]

During this trip, Grinnell made an interesting discovery about mountain sheep. Reynolds had told him that in spite of its name, this animal was commonly found in open country miles from buttes, badlands, or other elevations. Reynolds claimed in fact that sheep often fed with antelope far out on the prairie. Even though these statements disagreed with Grinnell's preconceived notions, he discovered their truth on the trip down the Missouri. While making a short side hunt, the two men encountered "a sheep feeding among the sage brush on the . . . River bottom. . . ."[37] Years later, Indians informed Grinnell that they had had similar experiences before the coming of the white man.[38]

On the second day of the downstream journey, Grinnell witnessed a scene featuring a mountain sheep that would remain burned in his memory. As their boat was gliding gently down river, and "the sun just topping the high Bad Land bluffs to the east, . . . a splendid ram stepped out upon a point far above the water, and stood there outlined against the sky. Motionless, with head thrown back, and in an attitude of attention, he calmly inspected the vessel floating along below him; so beautiful an object amid his wild surroundings, and with his background of brilliant sky, that no hand was stretched out for the rifle, . . . [and] the boat floated quietly on past him, and out of sight."[39]

"We spent two nights on the river, sleeping on the sand bars, and during our passage we saw no one, though we passed and examined a very recent Indian camp. Our practice was to land on the shore or a sand bar late in the afternoon, build a fire and cook our food, and then, after eating, to push off the boat and pass on down the river, landing again after dark on some other sand bar, where we slept.

"This second move was objected to by Ned Ludlow on the first night, who asked why it was necessary to go on. Charley Reynolds' reply was, 'I do not mind getting killed, but I should hate to have somebody come along next year and kick my skull along the sand and say, "I wonder what fool this was, who built a fire in this country and then slept by it." ' "[40]

After reaching Carroll, Grinnell and his companions rejoined the expedition, and "we went on down the river."[41] Arriving finally at Bismarck, Grinnell said good-bye to Charley Reynolds and boarded a train for the East. "I at once went home and found the family at Milford, where they remained until December, when they went to California."[42]

The 1875 Yellowstone expedition had several important results. Ludlow's report on the reconnaissance, which included sections on paleontology and zoology by Grinnell, and geology by Dana, "forms one of the best brief descriptions of the Park extant."[43] The trip also helped to solidify the Army's new role as the subsidizer of the more sophisticated, academic approach to Western exploration. Most significant of all, the journey aroused in Grinnell an interest in the future of Yellowstone Park, the genesis of his later campaign to define the status of the area and protect it from commercialization.

6

Collecting Artifacts, Fossils, and Trophies

WHEN GRINNELL RESUMED HIS DUTIES in the Peabody Museum, he found the staff feverishly laboring to examine and classify the great quantities of material Marsh was continually receiving from all parts of the country. "Through the early winter I worked in the Museum. . . . In January mother wrote me from Santa Barbara that father seemed rather lonely and dissatisfied in California. Sightseeing did not greatly appeal to him, and mother asked if I would go out there and make them a short visit in the hope that my presence would be of some help."[1] The family's objective in visiting Santa Barbara had been to improve the health of Grinnell's father, but as yet, his condition remained unchanged.

"It was not easy for me to make up my mind to give up my work [for Marsh] . . . , even temporarily; but obviously it was more important to be of use to my father than to follow my preferences as to my personal occupation. Accordingly, early in the year 1876 I stopped work in the Museum and came to Santa Barbara.

"I started in February and the trip across the continent was long, because the . . . Railroad was held up by heavy snows in the Sierra Nevada Mountains for two days. When our train reached the point [of] . . . the delay . . . , a line of several trains stood ahead of ours, waiting for the snow-plows to work their way through the drifts which blocked the railroad. Before the tiresome delay was over, the food in the dining-car had been consumed, and the needs of the passengers were supplied, in part, by bread and meat brought in baskets by men on foot from the nearest railroad station, seven miles distant.

"At last the trains broke through, and we finally reached San Francisco. At that time there was no railroad along the coast south of [that city] . . . , and the quickest way to reach Santa Barbara from the north was by steamer. . . . By this means I came South and found my family located in the Arlington Hotel, which was then at the border of the town. . . ."[2] "The family seemed to be having a very good time. Father had made some pleasant acquaintances, and distant cousins — the Ivisons — resided there; the girls spent much of the time in the saddle."[3]

"The town was then hardly more than a village, with but one principal street."[4] "The Morris House, the only hotel within the city limits, was badly kept and very uncomfortable; a company had put in a new hotel, the Arlington, . . . but when it was completed, they had no money left with which to furnish it. However, arrangements were made for furnishing a few rooms, into which our family had moved, taking their meals at the Morris Hotel or sometimes cooking them themselves.

"Before starting out, Marsh had commissioned me to dig, if possible, in some of the old Indian villages formerly occupied by the almost extinct Coast Indians. . . ."[5] "After meeting my family, seeing the local sights, and eating the February strawberries, which, of course, were a surprise to me, I began to make inquiries about these ancient village sites and learned something as to their location. No one seemed to know much about them or what they contained; and presently I tried to learn as to this. I made the acquaintance of a livery-stableman named George Hartley, and getting a team from him and a man to help me, I went out to a place called *Cienigitas* [sic].[6] There, for several days, I dug in the old village mounds and took out many pre-historic artifacts which I finally sent back to the Peabody Museum, where they were exhibited for many years and perhaps are still on view."[7]

Among the items Grinnell collected "were several gigantic ollas and some beautiful soapstone pipes, the mouth-pieces of which were bird bones set into the smaller opening of the cigar-shaped pipes by means of asphalt. We found few . . . if any stone implements of primitive type."[8]

"In company with one of the men I had hired to help me dig, I went one night to a Mexican house and saw there a woman who, I was told, was the sole survivor of a tribe of Indians removed by the Spaniards from one of the Channel Islands, perhaps San Nicolas. As the story ran, a vessel was sent by the Spanish fathers with the purpose of moving the surviving Indians to the mainland. A child was left behind, and its mother jumped overboard to return to it. She reached land and for many years lived there, alone. She supported herself on the products of the Island, largely sea birds and their eggs; made her own tools of bone or stone, and her dresses of the skins of birds. She lived there alone for eighteen years before she was discovered and brought to the mainland, in 1853. . . . The man who took me to see her told me that during her lonely sojourn on the Island, she had forgotten how to talk."[9]

"I have seen accounts stating that the woman did not live long after her capture, and if this is true, evidently I could not have seen her in 1876. The woman I saw was elderly, scarcely less than 65 or 70 years old. My memory of the occurrence is quite vague. . . .

"I returned from California the last of February, 1876, and was again detained by snows in the Sierra Nevada Mountains for two days."[10] As Grinnell's father was feeling better, "the family returned in the spring and went to Milford, where they spent the summer."[11]

Earlier, in May, Grinnell received a telegram from Custer inviting him to be his guest on a summer expedition into the land of the Sioux. The famed commander wanted the Army to continue supporting the new scientific approach to exploration, if it could be done without slowing down his reconnaissance. Grinnell's experience in the Western wilderness insured that he would be able to perform his work without special help from the military. The young patrician was particularly eager to go, since it meant another opportunity to be with his dear friend, Charley Reynolds.

But "at the time, we were extremely busy in the Museum with new material that was constantly being received, and it was thought also that on a military expedition such as this, there would be no opportunity to collect fossils nor even to search for new localities where collections might be made later."[12] With deep-felt regret, Grinnell acquiesced to Marsh and telegraphed Custer and Reynolds that he would be unable to meet them at Fort Lincoln on May 30, as requested.[13]

Seven weeks later, at his father's farm in Milford, he learned the fate of Custer and his men. A profusion of images from the past must have flashed through his mind as he thought of his slain friends and acquaintances in the 7th Cavalry. The evening on the Black Hills reconnaissance when he, North, and Reynolds talked of the possibility of a Sioux war must have come back in all its tragic irony. Most of all, he thought of Charley Reynolds.

If Grinnell had accompanied the expedition, he almost certainly would have been in the battle, for his close friendship with the scout meant that the two always rode together.[14] In the three-pronged assault on the village, led by Custer, Major Marcus A. Reno, and Captain Frederick W. Benteen, Reynolds happened to be with Reno's battalion, the first force to engage the Indians. After crossing the Little Bighorn, the Major's three companies were quickly repulsed by a storm of arrows and bullets. Reno gave the order to retreat back across the river. "The soldiers started with more or less order, but the fire was terrible, and in a moment they became panic-stricken and crowded toward the ford. A body of 500 Indians was charging toward them down the valley. Charley called out to the scouts, 'Here, boys, let us try to stop these Indians and give the soldiers a chance to cross.' The scouts stayed behind and turned, shooting into the charging mass, a dozen men against 500; the Indians came on like a whirlwind and struck. The soldiers crowded at the ford [and] . . .

were killed like sheep as they struggled to get across. They made no defense. They were butchered with bullets, arrows, lances and clubs, or knocked off their horses with gun barrels. 'It was like killing buffalo,' a Cheyenne who was in the charge [later] . . . said to me . . . .

"Charley's horse had been killed at once. He shot an Indian who was charging toward him on a buckskin pony, and as the Indian did not . . . fall off, he shot the horse, and Indian and pony rolled over together almost at his feet. He fired again, and then again. Bullets and arrows were flying thick. Suddenly Charley seemed to be hit in half a dozen places. He fell, raised himself on his elbow and fired another shot — his last. Then he sank back."[15]

Remaining in the East all that summer, Grinnell worked at New Haven through July, helping the Peabody Museum to clear away its work. From early August on, he was at Milford with the family. "At that time, summer shooting was lawful, and I killed a good many woodcock. That, with horseback riding and bota- nizing, made up most of my diversions. . . ."[16]

As already indicated, Grinnell had been using his spare time for several years to contribute to the new outdoor journal, *Forest and Stream*. Since its first issue, the paper had contained a "Natural History" section, making it probably the first weekly in the country to make this subject a regular feature. Charles Hal- lock, the editor and owner, quickly perceived that the column could be the periodical's most unique contribution, but he was handicapped by a paucity of expert advice. With "his scientific knowledge, which was fully abreast of the time," Grinnell filled the void.[17]

After becoming increasingly dissatisfied with the work of Ernest Ingersoll, the editor of the natural history column, Hallock fired him in the fall of 1876 and asked Grinnell to take the post.[18] Hallock emphasized that the paper was an important "vehicle of information" and that "its contributors and subscribers are among the leading men of this country and parts of Europe."[19] He also noted that "the ground occupied by the *Forest and Stream* is not elsewhere similarly filled."[20]

When Hallock agreed to let him continue his studies in New

Haven and write the feature by mail, Grinnell accepted. "I was to furnish a page or more of material weekly, to write reviews of natural history books, and generally to make myself efficient."[21]

Ironically, Hallock predicted that Grinnell would find the work so interesting that he would eventually leave New Haven and open a permanent office in New York City.[22] In less than four years Grinnell would do just that and, in the process, replace Hallock as the newspaper's editor, owner, and publisher.

"The winter of 1876–77 was spent quietly in New Haven, working at the Museum. Dr. E. S. Dana and I usually got together about 5 o'clock in the afternoon and — no matter what the weather — took a walk which lasted for an hour or more. Occasionally we walked in the evening, but usually we were too busy for that. I had writing to do, and Dana had other work; he was already busy with his father's publication, the *American Journal of Science,* on which he spent much time. . . ."[23]

With the arrival of summer, the Peabody Museum sent Grinnell to Greenfield and Turners Falls, Massachusetts, where he made casts of dinosaur footprints, known as "bird tracks" by the local inhabitants.[24] Later, "in response to an invitation from Luther H. North, I went out to western Nebraska to visit him. That spring, . . . William F. Cody and Frank North had gone into the cattle business, had bought a herd of Texans [longhorns] that had come up over the trail to North Platte City, and taken them out to turn loose in the wild country at the head of the Dismal River, which they claimed as their ranch. About the same time, other cattlemen came into the country. There was a ranch to the north of them on the middle Loup, . . . another to the west, . . . and several down along the Platte River. . . . At that time North Platte City was a typical cow town, and, during the arrival of the drives, was full of Texas cowboys, who often became noisy and sometimes quarrelsome.

"The 'ranch,' when I reached it, consisted of a couple of tents stuck up on the edge of the alkaline lake which was the head of the Dismal River. On this lake a pair of trumpeter swans had a nest. The sand hills roundabout abounded in antelope and deer. There were some elk in the country, and one or two little bunches of buffalo.

"While at the ranch I spent all my time with Lute, riding about with him over the country working the cattle, and incidentally hunting. Game was plenty, and we killed all that was needed at the ranch.

"During this visit Lute North gave an exhibition of his most extraordinary knowledge of the habits of the animals of the prairie. . . . Lute and I were riding up a long, wide valley on the lefthand side of which were high, steep sand hills. Scattered all over the valley were cattle and horses and mingled with them a few antelope, all of them distant and on the flat prairie. As we rode along talking, we saw the head and then the shoulders of an antelope appear on the top of a high bluff to the left, only 400 or 500 yards away. We checked our horses, slipped off them on the side away from the pronghorn, and lay down on the ground, watching the antelope. It stood there for a little time looking over the valley, seeing only the ordinary objects of the prairie: horses and cattle. Presently the antelope drew back from the top of the bluff and disappeared, and I grasped my rifle and prepared to try to stalk it. 'Hold on a minute,' said Lute, 'he'll be back before long.' Three or four moments elapsed, and then the buck's head was seen again, and he took another long look over the valley and again drew back. This was repeated twice more, and when the antelope had disappeared for the fourth time, Lute said, 'All right, now go ahead.' I hurried over on foot, climbed the bluff, and peering through the grass at the top, I saw the buck antelope and a doe standing broadside to me less than 100 yards away, sleepily chewing their cud. I shot carefully at the buck, and as the smoke blew away, I saw him come running almost directly toward me. Presently he passed, and I saw him go down the steep slope toward the valley and disappear. I walked toward the place, while Lute came on with the horses, and we found the buck dead. He was an extraordinarily large and fat antelope, so fat that when the blood cooled that came from him, it was full of little white globules of fat.

"It was years before I had any glimmering of comprehension of why Lute knew that this animal would come back three or four times to repeat his inspection of the valley, and I still think that the act showed extraordinary hunter's sense. It is possible that some act of the antelope as he turned away the last time may have told Capt. North, without his really knowing it, that the antelope was satisfied, but even today the mystery of that decision puzzles me."[25]

Another memorable hunting incident took place "one evening [as] one or two of the boys, [plus] Jim Carson, an old trapper who was stopping at the ranch, and Lute and myself were sitting near the main tent. . . . We saw a deer come up over the bluff half a mile distant and begin to feed down toward the valley, and at last disappear in the high grass and underbrush. Carson declared that he would go after it and took his rifle and set out. For a good distance we could see him, and then he disappeared. Soon after that, the deer left his concealment and began slowly to work along the face of the hill, so that we could see every move it made, but we did not know whether Carson was aware of the animal's change of position.

"Presently something seemed to alarm the deer and it started bounding up the hill. A shot came from Carson and a moment later another shot that I saw knock up the soil well in advance of the deer, which, after a jump or two more, fell and began to roll down the hill; a moment later Carson appeared from the bushes and began to butcher it.

"When he returned to camp, carrying the small deer on his shoulders, Lute North asked him why he had fired the second shot. Carson looked at him in some surprise and then replied: 'Because I wanted the deer.' 'Well,' said Lute, 'you got the deer with the first shot and missed him altogether with the second. There is only one hole in the deer, you see.' 'Nonsense,' said Carson, 'I missed him with the first shot and killed him with the second.' 'Not at all,' said Lute, 'I distinctly saw him flinch at the first shot, and we all of us here saw the second shot miss him. If you had held your fire a few moments longer, he would have rolled down to you just as he did, and you would have saved a cartridge.'

"Carson would not have it so. He was convinced that the second shot had been the effective one."[26]

Shortly after this incident, Grinnell returned to the East. The rest of the year 1877, "and the next two years as well, were devoted in great part to work on the Cretaceous collections, especially the *Odontornithes,* on which . . . Marsh began seriously to work. At this I helped him, . . . doing the work any assistant would have done. The volume was completed and finally published in 1880.[27]

"In the summer of 1878, say in July or August, I started west for a hunting and fossil collecting trip in the Rocky Mountains. The man I engaged to go with me was William H. Reed, afterward curator of fossils in the University of Wyoming. . . . I do not recall just how I came to know him, but it was probably in this way: W. E. Carlin, the station agent at Como, a stop on the Union Pacific Railroad about seven miles from Medicine Bow, came east, bringing with him two dinosaur vertebrae which he wished to sell to Marsh. He said that there were plenty more to be had at this place. Through Carlin, I think, Marsh heard of Reed, who Marsh hired to collect vertebrate fossils from the Jurassic exposures near Como.[28] I went out to look over the ground. This afterward became one of the great collecting grounds of North America for Jurassic fossils, and vast numbers of species have been described from the general region.

"Reed and I started from Como to go to Elk Mountain and beyond that to Wagonhound Creek, and we made quite a round. . . . Later my brother Mort joined us, and we stayed for some time at Como station, shooting ducks during the day, sleeping on the floor of the station at night, and on the whole having a very good time.

"Finally Mort went on to California while I returned east and stopped at North Platte City to go out to the ranch on the Dismal, where I worked for a time with the cattle."[29] By this time the Norths had built themselves a fine log house, built of cedar logs. Down the creek was a sod stable. The ranch house "was eighteen feet wide and thirty-six feet long. It was divided into two rooms, one being the kitchen and the other the living and sleeping room."[30]

"The Sioux Indians, from the various bands of Spotted Tail and Red Cloud, roamed over this country, which was their favorite hunting ground, and although they were peaceable . . . , Major North had his log house constructed with a view to protection, for the Indians were not always to be trusted and occasionally a hostile band might come down upon him unawares. Besides, the Sioux disliked Major North for the part he had taken against them as the leader of their enemies, the Pawnees, and he knew that they would soon learn of his establishing a ranch on the Dismal River.

"He accordingly had his men furnished with long-range guns and other arms, and a good supply of ammunition was stored in the house. Port-holes were made through the log walls on every side, so that the little fortress commanded the field in all directions. The corral and stable being located nearby were thus easily protected. The situation of the fortress was such that during the daytime Indians could not come within three-quarters of a mile of it, from any point, without being discovered. With all these precautions Major North felt secure from Indian raids."[31]

During that summer, Luther North and Grinnell had a friendly disagreement over a hunting trophy. "In the dry lakes of the sand hill country to the west of the ranch, there were many deer, and on one or two occasions we went over there to hunt them. The deer spent their time for the most part in the high grass, which was often up to the horses' heads, and as the horses in moving through this made much noise, the deer usually jumped up some distance ahead of the horsemen and ran off, presenting a very difficult mark for the rifle.

"At one of the lakes we had seen a gigantic deer once or twice but had never been able to get a shot at him. One morning Lute and I set out before daylight and reached the lake where this deer had been seen just as the sun was rising. We did not ride through the high grass but examined the open places, and finally discovered the great deer, and before long approached within rifle range. The animal was so large and had so superb a head that I was exceedingly anxious that it should be obtained, and distrusting my own shooting, I asked Lute to take the first shot. After some demur, he agreed, provided I would disregard him after he had fired, and this I promised to do. He shot and the buck bounded off toward the tall grass, but after I fired, it fell, and was almost dead when we reached him. After dressing the animal, it was all we . . . could do to lift it up and slip it over the tail of a rather small pony, so that it could be tied to the saddle.

"Lute congratulated me on having made a good running shot, while I insisted that it was his shot that had killed the deer and that I had missed it altogether."[32] As we have seen earlier, mortally wounded big game often run some distance before dropping. "Of course there was only one hole in the skin. In each case the animal had been almost broadside to the shooter, so that there was nothing to be learned from the position of the bullet hole, nor did the size of the opening at either point of entrance or exit settle the matter, and it never has been settled to this day. The deer . . . had the most symmetrical pair of antlers . . . I have ever seen, and at one of the Sportsman's Shows in New York [City] a number of years ago, the head was given the prize as the best white-tailed deer exhibited. It is now in the National Collection of Heads and Horns, in the custody of the New York Zoological Society, at the Bronx Park [Zoo]."[33]

It was the summer of 1878 "that I came in from the Cody and North ranch feeling pretty ill."[34] Grinnell did not know it then, but he had contracted what would prove to be an almost fatal case of Rocky Mountain spotted fever.[35] "We started in in the afternoon, rode about 20 miles . . . , stopped there and slept, and the next morning went on in. I had only a saddle blanket for covering and shivered and shook all night long, but supposed that this was because I was cold. The next day on the way in we passed a roundup wagon, and sometime in the middle of the next night, I took the train east at North Platte station. The last thing I had any clear memory of was passing the roundup wagon.

"During the four or five days that it took me to get back to Milford, Connecticut, I was quite ill, always delirious at night and weak and miserable during the day. I reached home barely able to totter, was met by my father at the bridge at Naugatuck Junction, and went to bed, where I remained for seven long weeks. For a good part of that time, I was out of my head . . . , and my delirium always took one form. I imagined myself riding about the cattle, saw great banks of clouds coming up in the west with thunder and lightning, and then the cattle would break away, and of course we would all ride after them as hard as we could.

"At length I began to eat the slops usually fed to sick people and gradually got up and started to walk about with a cane. Little by little, I began to go over to New Haven for an hour or two a day and finally recovered."[36]

Undaunted by his experience in Nebraska the previous year, Grinnell went West again in 1879. Leaving the Union Pacific Railroad in southeastern Wyoming, he and four companions traveled south into Colorado and through the high plateaulike valleys known as North and Middle Parks. Their journey would take them into the same region now occupied by Rocky Mountain National Park.

"Our party . . . left Laramie about three o'clock on a bright, pleasant Wednesday afternoon. . . . Two of the number, A. and W., had never before been west of the Missouri river, and so everything would be new to them.[37] Fuller, our teamster, and William, the cook, with the writer, made up the company. A stout team drew the Studebaker wagon which carried our provisions, bedding and ammunition, and three excellent saddle horses were provided for the accommodation of those who preferred riding to a seat in the wagon. . . .

"The first day's march took us to Leroy's [ranch] on the Laramie River, a distance of only seventeen miles."[38] The country was already full of cattle, sheep and goats, and in some areas, ranchers had erected fences to keep their cattle out of the hay fields along the . . . River.

"Ten or twelve miles from Laramie I noticed in the road, which at this point ran for some little distance close to one of these fences, the tracks of several antelope, and a mile or two further on we saw the animals themselves. They were evidently trying to get down to the water and were following the fence along, searching for an opening through which they might pass. So intent were they upon this that we rode up to within six or eight hundred yards of them before they saw us, and we might have approached still nearer to them had it not been for the wretched dog owned by our teamster, which as soon as it caught sight of the game started in hot pursuit. Of course he could not catch the antelope any more than a tortoise could catch a streak of lightning, but this 'Shep' did not know, and was never able to learn. The antelope did not pay much attention to him until he got to within about a hundred yards of them, and even then they merely cantered off slowly. When, however, he still gained rapidly on them and was soon only fifty yards behind the herd, they seemed to realize that he was chasing them. A little cloud of dust obscured the clump of fleeing beasts for a moment and then they emerged from it running, literally, like the wind. The dog seemed to be standing still, and, in less time than it takes to write it, the antelope were out of sight. . . .

"The sun was setting when we reached Leroy's, and by the time our tents were up and the animals fed it was quite dark. An early start was made next morning, as the march . . . we proposed to make was over thirty miles. I lingered behind to examine some fossils which had been found in the bluffs near the river and which were supposed to be of peculiar interest. The specimens proved to be the bones of the great Dinosaurian reptiles, which lived in such great numbers in this region during the Jurassic age. They were in good preservation, but did not appear to differ materially from specimens already in some of our eastern museums. I caught up with the team and the other riders just as they were leaving the river."[39]

Toward evening the men reached Beaver Creek and camped for the night, but with the dawn, they were off again. "Soon after leaving . . . the Beaver, we reached what is termed the Neck of . . . [North] Park, and passing over the divide, followed down a valley, at first narrow, but gradually becoming wider, which led us over a good though somewhat hilly road, toward a more open country. Two or three hours of riding brought us to Pinkham's ranche [sic], where the Park begins . . . .

"The country at this point had been burned over and was black and extremely desolate in appearance. I inquired the cause of the fire and learned from the owner of the ranche [sic] that the burn had been made to clear off the sage brush, which takes up so much room that might be occupied by grass. 'And then,' said my informant, 'the cattle won't graze where the sage brush is thick; they can't; the branches stick into their eyes and . . .

blind 'em.' When the sage has been burned off, it is usually followed the next season by a crop of grass . . . ."[40] Many people today think that the practice of periodically burning off the range to expand the food supply for domestic or wild animals is a recent development of scientific wildlife management, but Grinnell's experience shows that the procedure has been in use for some time.[41]

The thing that impressed Grinnell "more and more each year," in his travels beyond the frontier, was "the rapidity with which our western country is settling up."[42] For "as soon as any section becomes safe, the Indians having been driven off, the cattlemen begin to drive their herds into it, and before long, one hears complaints that there are too many cattle there. The older settlers complain that the [newcomers] . . . are 'crowding them,' and soon the most energetic commence to move off in search of 'fresh fields and pastures new.' "[43] Now the process was occurring in the North Park region; 6,000 head of beef were already on its range.[44] While the area still had abundant wildlife and even free-ranging hunting parties of Indians, Grinnell knew that all this was about to pass away.

As he traveled through North Park, he found that he had picked the right spot for his 1879 trip. He had come because "this region was . . . believed to be a great game country. So it proved."[45] While all the Western big-game species were encountered, the pronghorn antelope was present in incredible numbers. In the valley of the North Platte River, Grinnell and his companions saw pronghorn in all directions, everywhere, as far as the eye could see.[46] Whenever there was open country on the journey ahead, the explorers invariably discovered bands of fifty to sixty antelope dotting the prairie around them, often totaling many hundreds in any one area. In some places the animal's trails were "worn eight or ten inches deep in the hard soil."[47]

From where Grinnell's party made its first North Park camp, the Snowy Mountain Range lay ten or fifteen miles to the west. As Grinnell was considering taking the group through the mountains, he climbed the highest peak in the area to ascertain the best route. "But on reaching the summit, after a very hard pull,

I discovered that the whole range was on fire. Of course it was useless to look for game there. I was well repaid for my scramble up the hill, however, for in the valley at my feet, stretching away to the west for seven or eight miles, and to the north and south for fifteen, lay the largest beaver meadow . . . I have ever seen. I presume that there were 500 dams in sight, most of them kept in good repair. The water set back by these dams flowed through a thousand little canals and ditches, and the whole from the height looked like a silver net spread over an enormous carpet of emerald velvet. Through my glass I could count hundreds of beaver houses and could even distinguish the green willow leaves on the branches recently used in repairing the works. Beyond this meadow was a narrow strip of brown prairie, and then the green pine timber began, and with it the foothills of the Snowy Range. Deep dark gorges run up the mountain sides and seemed to promise an easy ascent; but the columns and masses of thick white smoke, which moved steadily along from the south toward where I sat looking, told me too surely that in a day or two at furthest, the fire would be sweeping over the whole range. Above the smoke I could see again the green timber, and above them the grim, grey rocks, bare of vegetation, and whitened a little higher up by patches of snow, pure and shining, when touched by the rays of the now sinking sun, but seeming grey and soiled when shaded by clouds. Turning to the eastward and looking out over the broad valley through which we had just come, the view was scarcely less impressive. From my eyrie I could count no less than twenty-two lakes of various sizes. Those furthest from me still gleamed in the sunlight like burnished silver, but the nearer ones, shaded by the towering peaks of the range, were dull and blue. With my glass I could just see upon the unruffled waters, little dots representing the water-fowl peacefully swimming hither and thither, and near the shores groups of antelope on their way from the water. Beyond the valley rose Independence Mountain, wooded to its summit, two-thirds of its height cold and hard in the shadow, but the summit still touched by the brilliant rays of the setting sun. A few moments and the light was gone. I turned for a last look at the snow-capped mountains, and how changed was the scene! The hillsides were now indistinct and blurred; but in the south, where an hour ago I had seen the white smoke, rose tongues of flame that seemed almost to lick the heavens, and beneath them the mountain-side was a red furnace that caused the sky to glow, and illumined the nearest snow-peaks with a roseate hue. The scene was one of beauty and grandeur, but its beauty was terrible and its grandeur filled me with awe. How long I stood gazing at this wonderful picture I do not know. I was recalled to myself by a furious storm of rain which began to fall, and picking up my rifle I slowly descended the mountain-side."[48]

"Very regretfully we turned our backs upon the Snowy Range and marched southeasterly toward the Platte River. The long stretch of rolling sage plain looked gray and gloomy under the heavy fog which hung low over the land, and which sometimes changed for a little while into a pouring rain, or again lighted up as though the sun were really trying his best to make things cheerful. . . .

"A low-lying mist produces a curious effect upon objects at a little distance. Antelope seen through the fog look as large as horses, and coyotes might easily be taken for gray wolves. The large size and hence apparent proximity of such living objects proved too great a temptation for our young men to withstand, and they indulged in a brisk fusilade [*sic*] at numerous antelope, none of which seemed any the worse for the firing. The fog seems . . . to confuse game at times. I had ridden ahead alone to pick out a road for the wagon and was loping up to the top of a low hill, when there appeared just over the ridge two antelope cantering briskly toward me. They did not seem to notice me until I was within a hundred yards of them, and then, instead of turning and running off, they put on a burst of speed and started to run directly by me, passing about thirty yards to my right. Just before they passed me I shouted at them, and one of the two turned and ran directly across my path so close to my horse that I thought I should run over him. I shouted at him again, just as he was in front of me, and he turned sharp to the left and darted by me, going like the wind. I could have struck him with a whip if I had had one, and had my rope been free, [I] would have thrown it over his head.

"Before noon the willowy bottom of the Platte was in sight,

and an hour's ride brought me to it, the wagon being far behind.
... We camped at this point and occupied the afternoon in collecting some natural history specimens....

"The next morning we crossed the Platte, and taking an easterly
course, reached the crossing of the Michigan about two o'clock
.... From the ... Michigan we took a hunter's road into the
mountains, which led us through dense pine forests alternating
with pretty park-like openings, about fifteen miles nearer to the
main range [of the Rockies], where we camped on some little
springs which flowed into the Canadian. Antelope were extraordinarily abundant here and quite tame, so that had we been
disposed to indulge in reckless killing, we might have done so
.... The day after our arrival at this camp, three of us rode over
to the Michigan to see a trapper [named Kosier] who was camped
on that stream, in order to make inquiries as to the best trail to
be followed in going up to the top of the range .... The trapper's
camp ... was rather picturesque in its ... surroundings, and extremely dirty. A light spring wagon containing most of the
owner's baggage stood between two trees, and over the wheels
hung saddles, bridles, ropes, and saddle blankets; nearby was a
smoking heap of ashes surmounted by a black and greasy pot;
and not far from the fire sat Kosier, skinning a beaver, while his
partner was pegging out a fresh antelope hide. The trees about
the fire were garnished with the circular pelts of the beaver, and
from two of them [were suspended] ... the ... drying carcasses
of a couple of antelope. We were hospitably received, and our
inquiries answered very cheerfully, and the visit resulted in our
engaging Kosier to go with us for fifteen days. He informed us
that the best trail to the top of the Range followed up the Michigan, and we decided to bring the wagon across from our camp
near the Canadian and leave it at Kosier's, whence we would
start with pack animals for our climb into the hills."[49] After bringing the wagon to the trapper's camp, the party proceeded along
the northern bank of the Michigan on their way to timber line.

They traveled "in single file, Kosier in the lead and the packs
near the head of the line. The valley became rapidly narrower
and rougher, and the impetuous force of the stream, which was
now only a brooklet, increased. Sometimes it fell down in a sheer

cascade for ten or fifteen feet, and at such points the trail would leave the stream and wind about in the timber until this ascent was overcome, when it would return to near the water's edge. Some of the slopes were very steep, and there were ... [many] dangerous places where a misstep on the part of one's horse would have thrown the rider down forty or fifty feet ... into the stream's bed below. . . . There was considerable down timber, which delayed us ..., for some of the logs were too large to be stepped over, and we were hence obliged to make considerable detours to get by them. At last, however, the valley through which we were traveling became a mere gorge, and after climbing a few hundred feet up a very steep slope we found ourselves at the edge of the timber. Only the forest ended here, however; a few stunted spruces flourished in the little ravines and sheltered nooks for 500 feet more of the ascent before finally giving up and acknowledging themselves vanquished by the Arctic climate. We paused at the foot of the open slope to allow those behind us to come up. . . ."[50]

After the party was all together again, "we approached the summit of the pass. The ascent was steeper than I had supposed, and our wearied horses had enough to do to drag themselves toward the top without carrying us . . . . The summit reached, we halted to rest and admire the scene before us. To the south and east we could see almost the whole of Middle Park, and all the rugged and broken mountains which surround it . . . .

"Continuing our march, we descended on the other side, . . . until we reached the first few spruces that grew highest up on this side of the range. Here we made camp, and soon afterwards I started out on foot to ascend the high mountain to the north and east of our camp. After reaching a point a few hundred feet above the level of the pass, vegetation almost ... disappeared, and a gray lichen, which attached itself to the loose blocks of trachyte which covered the ground, was the only plant to be seen. The mountain side was very steep, and the loose rocks afforded but an insecure foothold; besides this, the tenuity of the air was such that it was necessary to stop to take breaths at frequent intervals. Although an icy wind was blowing from the west, I was wet with perspiration by the time I reached the summit. Here I

reclined under the lee of a gigantic mass of rock, perfectly sheltered from the wind, and basked in the sunshine until I recovered
from the fatigue of my climb. Nearby was the edge of a beetling
precipice which almost overhung our camp, and repairing to this
I tried to estimate how high above my companions I was seated.
It was impossible for me to recognize, even with the help of my
excellent field-glass, any of my comrades in the camp; in fact,
it was difficult to see the individuals at all, except when they
moved. The horses grazing in a little meadow near the camp
looked smaller than so many setter dogs. I learned afterward that
those who saw me from camp took me for a mountain sheep, but
finally recognized what the moving object was by the glint of my
field-glass in the sun's rays. . . .

"Two days more were passed in this camp and occupied in
climbing the highest mountains and enjoying to the full their
majestic scenery. Game we found very scarce, prospectors and
Indians having driven it off. . . . At last our provisions gave out
and we were forced to turn our steps toward . . . [North] Park
once more, and a march of a day and a half brought us to
Kosier's camp."[51]

From Kosier's, the party traveled down the Michigan awhile
and then turned south. It crossed the Continental Divide through
Muddy Pass, going as far south as Hot Sulphur Springs.

"On our return journey we crossed the range by way of . . .
Rabbit Ears Pass [at 9,880 feet] and found the road a good one
. . . . Descending the mountains into North Park, we soon reached
a point where we could cross over and strike the road which we
had followed in going through . . . Muddy Pass. Near the point
where we struck this road, we passed a deserted Ute camp about
a month old, the poles of the wicky-ups [sic] and . . . the frames
for dressing hides being still in position.[52] The camp had not been
occupied for any great length of time, but I noticed several
bushels of antelope hair on the ground, indicating that the Indians
had dressed a large lot of skins."[53] "Here, too, we found remains
of old antelope traps put up by the Indians, the wings being
made of long rows of pine and cedar stumps which came together
in a V, no doubt leading to a pen or a pit in which the antelope
were to be enclosed."[54] Grinnell learned that during the summer

the Utes had "killed . . . thousands of antelope for their hides alone."[55] It appears that the Indian, once corrupted, could give up his customary reverence for nature and exploit it just as ruthlessly as the white man.

When Grinnell and his companions entered Colorado, they had heard a rumor that the Utes were in a "restless" mood. This news caused them a certain amount of anxiety and made the trip less than perfect. At it turned out, their fears were not unreasonable. Only a few days after the party left North Park, the Utes on the White River Reservation decided they had had enough of the whites' attempts to change their nomadic ways; they killed the agent, beseiged the reservation, and ambushed an army relief party of 160 men, killing the commander and thirteen others.[56] With the Custer debacle fresh in everyone's memory, all but a tiny minority of whites called for "teaching the Indians a lesson." Grinnell was one of the few who publicly asked that the Utes' position be seriously considered.[57] But the "Ute War of 1879" was the perfect excuse to subjugate the Indians and remove them from Colorado, and that is exactly what happened.

The day Grinnell and his comrades found the remains of the Indian village, the party camped on the east fork of Arapaho Creek. Before the trip ended, Grinnell hoped to bag one more trophy. That desire, plus the camp's need for fresh meat, resulted in his decision to make a hunt the next morning. Grinnell's poetic description of the hunt's beginning shows a feeling of oneness with the natural world that perhaps only sportsmen and naturalists ever obtain: "The day had not broken when I crawled out from my warm blankets into the frozen air. The grass and underbrush were white with frost; the gelid water which I dipped from the murmuring stream struck a chill to my very marrow as I quaffed it, and the heap of white ashes before our tents, reminding me of the genial warmth of last night's fire, made me shiver as I looked at it. The stars still shown with undiminished brilliancy, except in the eastern sky, where they were beginning to pale, and the surrounding mountains appeared like black amorphous piles, their outlines being scarcely distinguishable in the gloom.

"My preparations occupied but a few moments, and only stopping to light my pipe I trudged off into the darkness. There is a solitude, or perhaps a solemnity, in the few hours that precede the dawn of day which is unlike that of any others in the twenty-four, and which I cannot explain or account for. Thoughts come to me at this time that I never have at any other. Often I have experienced the mental state to which I refer, and the locality or situation has nothing to do with it. It comes when looking for the morning flight of ducks or geese in the populous East, just as it does while waiting for light to see deer in Nebraska, or when on some lofty peak of the Rocky Mountains I await the dawn to discover the whistling elk, or the bighorn cropping the tender grass on the steep hillside. Others, too, are influenced, I think, by some similar sensation, for when I have a companion with me at such a time he is usually subdued and quiet, and when he speaks, does so below his breath, as though afraid of breaking the universal stillness.

"As I moved from camp no sound broke the silence of the morning, save the cracking of the sage brush twigs as I brushed through them. Soon, however, it began to grow light, and with the dawn came the general awakening, and the quiet was broken by the voices of many a bird and beast. The coyotes commenced their doleful concert, a prairie dog or two barked, and the little striped [chipmunk] . . . squeaked in anger or alarm as he scuttled away from my path."[58]

The hunt was successful, the prize being a beautiful pronghorn buck. After bagging the antelope, Grinnell returned to his companions, and together they pushed on to their old campsite on Beaver Creek. From there, "we proceeded toward Laramie, making no lengthened stops by the way."[59] After reaching the town, a day was spent in "packing our collections and preparing for our journey east. I ran up on the evening express to Como, where I saw my good friend, [W. H.] Reed, and after a pleasant chat with him, all too short, took the morning train for the East."[60]

When Grinnell arrived back in New York, he found that the long brewing disunity in the *Forest and Stream* office was now at the boiling point. "During the two or three years past, I had from time to time purchased a few shares of *Forest and Stream* stock, and my father at one time had purchased . . . something over one-third of the capital stock, so that practically we had control. Mr. Hallock, president of the company, had become more and more eccentric, drinking heavily and neglecting his duties to the paper. The part-time treasurer and large stockholder, Mr. E. R. Wilbur, was disgusted with Hallock's course and used to complain about it to me, so that he and I, in the . . . frequent interviews we had, had come to know each other quite well.

"For some years I had been suffering from an inability to sleep, accompanied with many headaches,"[61] the result in part of his rigorous labors for Marsh and the Peabody Museum. "I consulted various doctors, without much satisfaction, but finally went to a Dr. Hammond in New York [City] who had a reputation as a nerve and brain specialist. He examined me, and after two or three interviews, during which he performed a variety of experiments, he told me that I must either change my work or be prepared to move into a lunatic asylum or the grave. During the winter of 1879–80, Wilbur had proposed that I should come to New York [City] and become president of the Forest and Stream Publishing Co., and after much consideration and many throes, I agreed to do this."[62] It was a monumental decision for the history of conservation.

"Before leaving New Haven, I passed examinations in osteology and vertebrate paleontology and received the Ph.D. at the commencement of 1880."[63] His dissertation was on "The Osteology of *Geococcyx californicus*" (road runner). "I left New Haven with keen regret, for I had hoped to work for a long time in the [Peabody] Museum.

"Prior to the annual meeting of the Forest and Stream Publishing Co., . . . Hallock had been told that he would not be reelected president of the company and after some objection had consented to give up his position and sell his stock. Charles B. Reynolds [no relation to Charley Reynolds] became managing editor, and on going to New York [City] I went into the office of *Forest and Stream*, then in the old Times Building in Park Row. At that time T. C. Banks was the secretary, John Banks the bookkeeper and cashier, Fred Mather the angling editor, C. P. Kunhardt the yachting editor, Franklin Satterthwaite the kennel editor, and Josiah Whitley the rifle man. It was an office full of competent people."[64] As editor in chief, Grinnell naturally supervised, in an overall way, the publication of the journal; from the beginning, however, he took personal charge of the natural history column and the editorial section. "We printed a good paper, had a large circulation, and began almost at once to make plenty of money, but it took some little time to pay off the debts incurred in previous years."[65] This effort was aided by the fact that "in the winter of 1880–81, . . . E. R. Wilbur retired from active business and came to *Forest and Stream's* office to be its active treasurer and business manager . . . . He soon began a reorganization of the business side of the paper which was very effective."[66]

Grinnell's new duties kept him from going west that year, but when the summer of 1881 arrived, he was eager to make a trip. The trouble was that his former "stamping grounds" — the Dismal River of Nebraska, the Black Hills of Dakota, the North Park area of Colorado, or any of the others — were being transformed beyond recognition by an invasion of prospectors, hide hunters, cattlemen, and farmers. Grinnell made up his mind to see country that was still unspoiled, even if it meant going outside the United States. He chose the western coast of Canada.

"Mr. A. H. Barney, at that time president of the Northern Pacific Railroad Co., asked me if I did not want to go out over the line of the road and see the region they were building through. He said that if I cared to go, he would 'chalk my hat' [pay all expenses]. I was glad of the opportunity to do this, and when the matter was suggested, Mr. Barney consented that Dr. E. S. Dana and Mr. E. H. Landon [a relative of Grinnell's] should go along."[67] They decided, however, to save this part of the trip for the return journey, for they were anxious to get to Canada as soon as possible.

"We went out over the Union Pacific Railroad to San Francisco, stopping on the way, I remember, at Como [Wyoming], Salt Lake City, and Lake Tahoe."[68] At the first place Grinnell visited his friend and fellow fossil-collector, W. H. Reed, and together they rode over the prairie to Como Bluff, where they spent the afternoon examining the fossil quarry and climbing the surrounding hills.[69]

Reboarding a Union Pacific train, Grinnell continued on his way to San Francisco. From there, "we purposed to go up the

California coast to British Columbia, where I had correspondents, J. C. Hughes and John Fannin, both interested in natural history and old hunters.[70] When we reached San Francisco, we discovered that a boat would leave in a day or two for Victoria and another one a few days later. As I had been in San Francisco before, it seemed best that I should go on by the first boat and try to arrange for an excursion in British Columbia, while Dana and Landon should spend a few days seeing the sights of the city, and then follow on, meeting me in Victoria. This plan was carried out.

"I went to Victoria and . . . after a night or two at the Driard House [Hotel], I crossed over to New Westminster, at the mouth of the Fraser River. Here I met Mr. Hughes, who a little while afterward took me over to Burrard Inlet and introduced me to Fannin, who had a cobbler's shop there.

"Hughes took me deer hunting on Mirror Lake, and we got a buck, and at Burrard Inlet I saw my first white [mountain] goat, high up on the mountain, and killed a black bear. At New Westminster I saw them catching and packing salmon, a wholly novel sight. With Hughes and Fannin I talked over the proposed trip, and they gave me letters addressed to Government people in Victoria, which was then a small place. I returned there, and presently Dana and Landon turned up, and we presented our letters. Through the kindness of certain men there, the sergeant of police — the head of the police force on the Island — was given thirty days leave of absence to go with us. We hired a cook, a white man known as Arizona Charlie, and a few days later took the steamer for Nanaimo. We carried with us our provisions, arms and blankets, and at Nanaimo, after a little trouble, we secured a large Chinook canoe and two Indians, one as bowman and one as steersman, the five white men agreeing to be the propelling power for the boat . . . .

"The scenery of the southern British Columbia inlets is among the most marvelous I have seen. . . . We worked hard on this trip, which covered about 600 miles, for we went up the various waterways as far north as the head of Bute Inlet.

"Returning, we went to Portland, Oregon. . . ."[71] From this point, Grinnell and his companions took a steamer up the Columbia. After a detour around the rapids at Cascade, the party continued by ship to The Dalles. Then, by various means of travel, the group reached the first construction camps of the Northern Pacific. "At that time the end of track building eastward was on the Spokane River, near Spokane Falls, where there was a tiny little village which is now the great city of Spokane."[72]

"With letters from one of the officials of the railroad, we left Spokan [sic] before light . . . for Lake Pend d'Oreille [sic]. Thirty-five miles of railroad travel brought us to Westwood, the end of the track, and there we took [a] stage for the lake."[73]

Soon they came to a huge railroad construction camp, "a veritable canvas city, and its inhabitants white men, Chinamen, horses, mules and dogs."[74] The Easterners passed "first the carpenters and bridge-builders, next the graders, and then the 'right of way men,' whose business it is to chop their way through the forest, and clear off all the timber along the line of the track for a width of fifty feet."[75] Once felled, the quickest way to get rid of the trees was to set them on fire. As often as not, the flames spread out of control and burned up much of the surrounding countryside. Appalled by this practice, Grinnell publicly attacked the railroad shortly after his return. "This is . . . the fault of the contractor," he wrote in *Forest and Stream*, "and there should certainly be some steps taken toward putting a stop to such . . . wanton destruction of valuable timber."[76]

Conditions had gotten so bad that the party's trip into Lake Pend Oreille actually became dangerous. "As we approached the lake, the woods were on fire everywhere. This had been going on for some time, and on several occasions, . . . the fires had been so extensive that the stages had been obliged to abandon all hopes of getting through. We were not stopped by the fire, although on several occasions we were obliged to drive between great piles of blazing logs, which made it unpleasantly warm for us."[77]

From the lake, the party proceeded to a place fifteen miles down the Pend Oreille River: Siniaqueateen, "a small settlement consisting only of a trading store, trader's house, and two or three storehouses and offices belonging to the railroad."[78] This was "the Northern Pacific Commissary depot for the supply of the engineer parties . . . laying out the line of the road over the Coeur D'Alene mountains. . . . I had a letter to Mr. Galbraith, the Commissioner of the company, who very kindly promised to provide us with the necessary outfit for our journey over the mountains."[79]

Siniaqueateen is an aboriginal word meaning, according to Grinnell, "the place where we cross."[80] For untold generations, it was here that Indians had forded the river on their travels north or south through the country. At the time of Grinnell's visit, there were many red men in the area. "One morning, as I stood out in front of the Indian camp, a Kootenai woman came along, driving in a bunch of horses she had just gathered. Hanging to her saddle-bow, in a baby board, was an infant, and on her back was another. The fact that they seemed to be twins made me look closely at them, and I noticed that they were very young. I spoke about them to Galbraith. He asked an Indian standing nearby, and then turned to me and said, 'Oh yes, they are twins; they were born this morning.' "[81]

"At Galbraith's camp I purchased, for $10.00 each, two of the handsomest bear skins I ever saw, one a grizzly, the other a black bear. Both of them were what might be called silk robes."[82]

"On leaving the Siniaqueateen for the lake, the river gradually becomes more and more wide, and the scenery is very attractive .... On our way ... we saw a number of Indians in their canoes."[83] The latter were "curious structures, made of the bark of the white pine, and sharply pointed at both ends."[84]

Berries grew abundantly around the lake, and the Indians of the region depended heavily on the dried fruit as a winter food supply. "On some islands in Lake Pend d'Oreille I found several small log houses filled with reed sacks, each of which contained a bushel of dried berries."[85]

"We crossed the lake in a sailboat, and with our bedding and gear, were landed at the railroad camp at the mouth of the Clark Fork [River]."[86] "A day or two was spent here ... getting the animals shod, the saddles together and our mess outfit ready, and then one bright morning a little train of seven animals filed out of the camp and took the trail for Missoula."[87] Following up the Clark Fork and then traveling overland, the party used a week to complete the trip.

After reaching Missoula, "we spent the night, and the next day took the stage for Deer Lodge. The stage ride was long, the last of it over mountains covered with snow and through very cold weather. We reached Deer Lodge in the early morning, before anyone was up, and we spent an hour or two thawing ourselves out before the stove, while we talked with the hotel porter who was just out of bed."[88]

The service in these frontier "hotels" was a bit different from what Grinnell was used to in the East. "While sitting there, we heard shouts from one of the rooms ranged along the hall on the ground floor, and presently a door opened and a man thrust out his head and called loudly, 'Porter, Porter!' 'What is it?' answered the porter. The guest said, 'I wish you to bring me a pitcher of water.' The porter replied, 'You will find plenty of water in the barrel at the end of the hall,' and resuming his conversation with us, he said, with an air of mild curiosity, 'I wonder if that pilgrim thinks I am paid $40.00 a month and board to pack water for *him?*'

"In Deer Lodge on this occasion I learned of the capture of a number of white [mountain] goats not long before and saw a photograph of one of them. . . . It was only just about this time that sportsmen and naturalists began to realize that the white goat was to be found in the United States in considerable numbers.

"From Deer Lodge we took a stage to Melrose, then the end of the narrow gauge railroad running north into Montana from . . . Utah. The man who handled the reins I afterwards knew very well as stage driver in Yellowstone Park. Later he took part in a stage robbery there and was arrested, convicted, and sent to Deer Lodge [prison] for a year. . . . He was known as 'Long Red,' probably because he wore long red chin-whiskers, and as 'Handsome Charley,' a name which may have been applied satirically. When we left Deer Lodge I remember that Charley was very drunk, as were several of the passengers. The stage was crowded full and the top covered with more people. It was a gruesome ride."[89]

From Melrose, "six days of continuous travel by rail brought us to New York."[90] "We reached home sometime in September . . . ."[91]

The end of the journey was also the end of a decade of experience in the Great West. What Grinnell saw on his 1881 trip reinforced a prediction he made two years before: "As I look back on the past . . . years . . . ," he wrote in 1879, "I can form some idea of the transformations which time . . . will work in the appearance of the [Western] country, its fauna, and its flora. The enormous wealth contained in the rock-ribbed hills will be every year more fully developed. Fire, air, and water working upon earth, will reveal more and more of the precious metals, [as well as] . . . the baser ores, now neglected . . . , but not less valuable from an economic point of view. Towns will spring up and flourish, and the pure, thin air of the mountains will be blackened and polluted by the smoke vomited from the chimneys of a thousand smelting furnaces; the game, once so plentiful, will have disappeared with the Indian; railroads will climb the steep sides of the mountains and wind through their narrow passes, carrying huge loads of provisions to the mining towns, and returning trains will be freighted with ore just dug from the bowels of the earth; the valleys will be filled with fattening cattle, as profitable to their owners as the mines to theirs; all arable land will be taken up and cultivated, and finally the mountains will be stripped of their timber and will become simply bald and rocky hills. The day when all this shall have taken place is distant no doubt, and will not be seen by the present generation; but it will come."[92] The sweep of Grinnell's prophecy is almost uncanny, and in his doubts concerning the beneficence of "progress," he would have much in common with environmentalists today.

Epilogue

During the late 1870's and early '80's, the Far West experienced a boom in the cattle business that lured thousands into ranching. Not wanting to be left out, Grinnell decided that he too would become a ranchman. At first he considered establishing a "spread" near the Cody-North ranch in Nebraska, but with the start of the new decade, stockmen drove their herds into the Dismal River area in such numbers that the range rapidly deteriorated. When homesteaders followed upon the ranchers' heels, Grinnell's friends realized that the days of the open range were almost at an end. As the land had lost its attraction, they sold their ranch in 1882 and retired from the frontier.[1]

Attempting to profit from the experience of Cody and the North brothers, Grinnell located his spread further west, in a region that he hoped would not soon be overrun by homesteaders. "In the spring of 1883 I purchased from Jamieson & Picard the sheep ranch they had established two or three years before in the Shirley Basin in southeastern Wyoming. I had hunted in the Basin and regarded it as one of the most attractive spots in the country.

Jamieson & Picard had a claim there on which were erected ordinary ranch buildings. They had 3,000 sheep and a few horses
. . . . I took possession of the 1,100 acres in April and went out again in the summer. . . ."[2] Grinnell engaged his old friend, William H. Reed, "as my superintendent, and hired two other men as helpers.

"My ranch project proved a financial failure. The altitude of the . . . Basin was about 7,500 feet, and the first winter I lost one-third of the sheep. I sold the remainder the next summer and put the money into horses and cattle. The horses did well, but not the cattle. The altitude was too great for anything except horses.

"After a few years I discharged my men and leased the place to Massengale and Ross, who took care of the stock. They kept the ranch for eight or ten years and then moved out of the country, and I hired Billy Collins to look after it."[3]

Despite the large amount of money put into the ranch, Grinnell took only a secondary interest in it from the start. He was too busy exploring in regions where solitude and freedom were often his sole companions. On an 1885 pack trip, he first entered the St. Mary's country of northwestern Montana, one of the wildest places left in the United States. Concentrating his attention on the eastern slope of the Continental Divide, he returned year after year, climbing the tallest mountains and finding the sources of the largest streams. He walked ground never before trod by any known white man, and most of the names he gave to the area's topography still remain in what is now Glacier National Park.[4]

What the romantic Easterner was seeking in the wilderness is revealed in a letter written many years later. "There is a great change between [now] . . . and old times in Montana and Wyoming," he told a friend in 1916.[5] "One might . . . as well live in Ohio or Illinois as in either of those states. The old charm is gone, for the old independence is gone."[6]

As PROGRESS reached into the Shirley Basin, Grinnell's interest in his Wyoming land diminished accordingly. Even in the early years on the ranch, he spent much of his time reminiscing about the past with his hired hands. One of these was "Scout," a former mountain man. On a hot September morning in 1883, he stirred his employer when he "fell into a revery in which his mind went back to other distant days. To a time when no railroad had brought civilization into these hills and when Nature was sole mistress here. When the valley below was dotted with the black buffalo. When the rocks among which he was now resting were the feeding ground of the bighorn; when there were among these pines a hundred elk and deer where now one is found, and when the red masters of the soil made their camps here, uncontaminated by the white man's vices, and undisturbed by his uncontrollable greed for their hunting grounds. To days when he and one or two companions would make their semi-annual visits to old Fort Laramie for ammunition and supplies, and would spend the remainder of the year far in the mountains, hunting and setting their traps, leading a peaceful and contented life, wishing for nothing more than the rock-ribbed hills yielded them. 'And now,' sadly thought the dreamer, 'I have to chop logs, or drive team, or punch cows for $30 a month and board. . . . Better to have been killed in some Indian fight than to have fallen to this.' "[7]

When the old mountain man had finished his lament, Grinnell reflected on him and his words: "Scout was one of few surviving relics of the days when the region west of [the] Missouri was truly the Far West, a class of men who have almost disappeared, and yet who were, in their day, characteristic of this wild country, and were its only white inhabitants. They have disappeared with the buffalo they used to hunt, and the Indians they used to fight. On this broad continent there is no longer a place for them."[8]

In comparison with Scout, Grinnell was a latecomer to the West; yet he had intimate knowledge of what the old man was talking about. As a twenty-year-old "pilgrim," he had left Omaha in 1870 when the country a hundred miles closer to the setting sun was the domain of the Sioux and Cheyenne. He had ridden through herds of bison when that animal numbered in the millions.

Now, merely thirteen years later, the "wild" Indians had been killed, or huddled on reservations, and the buffalo's population could be counted in the hundreds.[9] In what seemed like the blink of an eye, the twin symbols of the virgin West had vanished, thousands of square miles had been transformed, and Grinnell was still only a young man of thirty-three! While a number of factors would go into making him the great conservationist and ethnologist he later became — the assimilation of his father's ethical code, the acquisition of his uncle's sporting and natural history interests, the reinforcement of those interests by the Audubons, and the broad perspective given by the new academic sciences—none would be as important as the fact that in a little more than a decade, he had witnessed the passing of the Great West.

Notes

INTRODUCTION

1. Grinnell to Miss H. B. Audubon, January 13, 1916, Letter Book, pp. 665-66. Grinnell's letter books, formerly in the possession of the Connecticut Audubon Society, were transferred to Yale University in 1984. Arranged chronologically, each volume has approximately one thousand pages of copied letters. Thirty-eight books in all, they extend, with few gaps, from August 2, 1886 to October 17, 1929.

Interestingly enough, *Wikis*, the Cheyenne word for "bird," is the name of the "Indian" who recounts his early life in Grinnell's famous book, *When Buffalo Ran*, first published by Yale in 1920.

2. Margaret Mead and Ruth L. Bunzel, *The Golden Age of American Anthropology* (New York, 1960), pp. 113–14.

3. Grinnell, *The Cheyenne Indians: Their History and Ways of Life*, ed. Mari Sandoz (New York, 1962), p. v.

4. *Great Falls* (Montana) *Tribune*, November 18, 1936; Grinnell to Luther H. North, May 25, 1889, Letter Book, p. 328A; Grinnell to Hamlin Garland, November 26, 1897, *Ibid.*, p. 181; Grinnell to Herbert Welsh, November 10, 1898, *Ibid.*, p. 950.

5. C. H. Merriam to Grinnell, February 8, 1902, George Bird Grinnell Collection of Journals, Field Notes and other Materials on the Plains Indians, 1870–1930, Southwest Museum Library, Los Angeles, California, item no. 206; hereinafter cited as the Grinnell Collection. Grinnell to Mer-

riam, February 19, 1902, Letter Book, p. 151; Theodore Roosevelt to Grinnell, April 28, 1902, Roosevelt Papers, Library of Congress, Series 2; George Kennan to Grinnell, April 28, 1902, Grinnell Collection, item no. 170; Grinnell to Merriam, April 30, 1902, Letter Book, p. 351; Grinnell to S. M. Brosius, April 30, 1902, *Ibid.*, p. 352; Grinnell to Roosevelt, May 1, 1902, *Ibid.*, p. 374; Grinnell to Emerson Hough, May 2, 1902, *Ibid.*, p. 377; Grinnell to Garland, May 7, 1902, *Ibid.*, p. 395; "STANDING ROCK AGENCY, FORT YATES, N. DAK. MAY 23, 1902. MEMORANDUM AGREEMENT. Negotiated by GEORGE BIRD GRINNELL...," Grinnell Collection, item no. 549; Roosevelt to Grinnell, June 13, 1902, Roosevelt Papers, Series 2; "THE STANDING ROCK INDIANS AND THE GRAZING LEASES. Indian Rights Association. June, 1902," Grinnell Collection, item no. 206.

Grinnell to George B. Cortelyou, October 24, 1902, Letter Book, p. 575; Willis Fletcher Johnson, ed., *Addresses and Papers of Theodore Roosevelt* (New York, 1909), pp. 97–98; Grinnell to John Pitcher, December 8, 1904, Letter Book, p. 244; "The President's Message," *Forest and Stream* 63 (December 17, 1904): 505.

Grinnell to Roosevelt, November 17, 1904, Letter Book, pp. 191–92; Grinnell to Francis E. Leupp, November 21, 1904, *Ibid.*, p. 208; Grinnell to Pitcher, December 8, 1904, *Ibid.*, p. 244; Grinnell to "The President," October 31, 1912, *Ibid.*, p. 467.

6. *New York Times*, April 12, 1938.

7. See, for example, "Pure Air and Pure Water," *Forest and Stream* 54 (June 30, 1900): 501, and Grinnell to Fred Walcott, December 14, 1921, Letter Book, p. 965.

Grinnell's central role in the conservation movement up to 1901 is documented in my *American Sportsmen and the Origins of Conservation* (New York, 1975). For an outline of Grinnell's later activities in this area, see James B. Trefethen's *Crusade for Wildlife: Highlights in Conservation Progress* (Harrisburg, Pennsylvania, 1961), pp. 97-109, 150-78, 206-84, and 325-28.

CHAPTER ONE. GROWING UP WITH THE AUDUBONS

1. The name was originally spelled variously as Grenell or Grennell.

2. *New York Times*, April 12, 1938; *New York Herald Tribune*, April 12, 1938.

3. Grinnell to Frank G. Page, September 15, 1926, Letter Book, pp. 421–22; *Forest and Stream* 37 (December 24, 1891): 445.

4. Grinnell to Page, September 15, 1926, Letter Book, p. 422.

5. Grinnell, "MEMOIRS," p. 4. This typewritten, unpublished autobiography was written between November 26 and December 4, 1915, and covers his life up to 1883; the manuscript abruptly ends in the middle of a word on page 97. It is part of a huge mass of miscellaneous material pertaining to Grinnell formerly located in a metal filing cabinet in the library of the Birdcraft Museum. Hereinafter, this depository, which was transferred to Yale University in 1984, will be cited as the Grinnell File, though the MEMOIRS will be cited separately.

6. MEMOIRS, p. 6. The land for Central Park was acquired by the city in 1856.

7. MEMOIRS, pp. 6–7.

8. The editor has been unable to discover Cossett's Christian name. When known, the first name of persons mentioned in the text will always be given.

9. MEMOIRS, 8–9.

10. *Ibid.*, p. 5.

11. *Ibid.*, p. 11.

12. *Ibid.*

13. *Ibid.*, p. 10. Lucy Audubon was the painter's widow.

14. Francis Hobart Herrick, *Audubon the Naturalist; A History of his Life and Times* (New York, 1917) 2:309.

15. Grinnell, *Audubon Park: The History of the Site of the Hispanic Society of America and Neighboring Institutions* (New York, 1927), pp. 1–22.

16. *Ibid.*, p. 18.

17. *Ibid.*, pp. 12–13. Presumably one of Grinnell's ancestors acquired the bow from the Indians. "Saratoga" is probably Saratoga County, New York.

18. Grinnell, *Audubon Park*, p. 13.

19. Grinnell, "Recollections of Audubon Park," *Auk* 37 (July, 1920): 375.

20. MEMOIRS, p. 13.

21. For an account of the passenger pigeon's demise, see Peter Matthiessen, *Wildlife in America* (New York, 1959), pp. 119–21 and 158–61.

22. MEMOIRS, p. 13.

23. *Ibid.*, p. 15.

24. *Ibid.*, pp. 17–18. Despite the country atmosphere, New York City already had a population in excess of 813,000.

25. MEMOIRS, p. 19.

26. *Ibid.*, pp. 19–20.

27. *Ibid.*, pp. 20–21.

28. *Ibid.*, p. 23.

29. *Ibid.*, pp. 23–26.

30. By "fish hawk," Grinnell is probably referring to the osprey.

31. MEMOIRS, pp. 27–30.

32. *Ibid.*, p. 30. By "barbel," Grinnell probably means a member of the sucker family (*catostomidae*).

33. MEMOIRS, pp. 30–32.

34. *Ibid.*, p. 32.

35. *Ibid.*, p. 18.

36. Grinnell, "Recollections of Audubon Park," p. 373.

37. MEMOIRS, pp. 18–19.

38. *Ibid.*, p. 12.

39. *Ibid.*, p. 19.

40. Herrick, *Audubon the Naturalist* 2:300. Grinnell was reminiscing to Herrick.

41. *Audubon Magazine* 1 (February, 1887–January, 1888):196.

42. Grinnell, "Recollections of Audubon Park," pp. 375–76.

43. MEMOIRS, p. 19.

44. Grinnell, "Recollections of Audubon Park," p. 379.

45. Interview with John P. Holman, March 11, 1969.

46. MEMOIRS, p. 19.

47. Herrick, *Audubon the Naturalist* 2:255–56.

Because of its almost universal use, I frequently employ the term "buffalo," even though I am aware that "bison" is technically the only correct name for the wild cattle of North America. For the same reason, I later use the term "antelope," even though the pronghorn is not a true antelope.

The great auk is an extinct bird.

48. MEMOIRS, p. 27.

49. Grinnell to Jesse Monroe, December 27, 1911, Letter Book, p. 681.

50. MEMOIRS, pp. 32–33.

51. *Ibid.*, p. 33.

52. *Ibid.*

53. *Ibid.*

54. *Ibid.*, p. 34.

55. *Ibid.*

56. *Ibid.*

57. *Ibid.*, pp. 34–35.

58. Grinnell to E. S. Dana, August 21, 1908, Letter Book, p. 702.

59. Charles Schuchert and Clara Mae LeVene, *O. C. Marsh, Pioneer in Paleontology* (New York, 1940), pp. 97–99.

60. MEMOIRS, pp. 36–37. In various states the "chancellor" is the presiding judge of the court of chancery or equity.

61. Schuchert and LeVene, *O. C. Marsh*, pp. 297–98.

62. MEMOIRS, p. 37.

63. Grinnell, "An Old-Time Bone Hunt," *Natural History* 23 (1923): 330.

CHAPTER TWO. REDISCOVERING THE WEST

1. William H. Goetzmann, *Exploration and Empire: The Explorer and the Scientist in the Winning of the West* (New York, 1966), p. 429. Even though the Marsh explorations were not military expeditions, they had military escorts, as did other scientific expeditions of the period.

2. Schuchert and LeVene, *O. C. Marsh*, p. 102.

3. Grinnell, "An Old-Time Bone Hunt," *Natural History* 23 (1923): 330.

4. MEMOIRS, pp. 37–38.

5. *Ibid.*, p. 38.

6. Grinnell to P. J. McGill, January 18, 1892, Letter Book, p. 713; Grinnell to E. W. Nelson, May 11, 1916, *Ibid.*, p. 116.

7. Grinnell to F. G. Webber, January 22, 1892, *Ibid.*, p. 727.

8. Grinnell, "William Cody," Grinnell File, pp.1–4.

9. MEMOIRS, p. 38.

10. Grinnell, "An Old-Time Bone Hunt," p. 330.

11. Grinnell to Arnold Hague, May 8, 1900, Letter Book, p. 885.

12. MEMOIRS, pp. 38–39.

13. Grinnell, "An Old-Time Bone Hunt," pp. 330–32.

14. MEMOIRS, p. 39.

15. Grinnell, "An Old-Time Bone Hunt," p. 332.

16. Grinnell to "My dear Father and Mother," August 3, 1870, Grinnell File.

17. *Ibid.* Lieutenant Bernard Reilly, Jr., was co-commander of the 5th Cavalry escort.

18. Grinnell to "My dear Father and Mother," August 3, 1870, Grinnell File.

19. *Ibid.* Charles McCormick Reeve, Yale class of 1870, later served in the Minnesota state legislature and became a colonel in the 13th Minnesota Volunteers during the Spanish-American War; in 1908 he was promoted to brigadier general.

20. Grinnell to "My dear Father and Mother," August 3, 1870, Grinnell File.

21. *Ibid.*

22. Lieutenant Earl D. Thomas was co-commander of the 5th Cavalry escort.

23. Grinnell to "My dear Father and Mother," August 3, 1870, Grinnell File.

24. Grinnell, "An Old-Time Bone Hunt," p. 333.

25. *Ibid.*

26. MEMOIRS, p. 39.

27. Grinnell to Arnold Hague, May 8, 1900, Letter Book, p. 885.

28. MEMOIRS, p. 39.

29. Grinnell to Arnold Hague, May 8, 1900, Letter Book, p. 886.

30. John Reed Nicholson, Yale class of 1870, was later chancellor of Delaware.

31. Grinnell to "My dear Father and Mother," August 26, 1870, Grinnell File.

32. *Ibid.*

33. MEMOIRS, pp. 39–40.

34. Grinnell to "My dear Father and Mother," August 26, 1870, Grinnell File.

35. *Ibid.*

36. *Ibid.*

37. MEMOIRS, p. 40.

38. A "saw duck" is a merganser.

39. Grinnell to "My dear Father and Mother," August 26, 1870, Grinnell File.

40. *Ibid.*

41. MEMOIRS, p. 41.

42. Grinnell to "My dear Father and Mother," August 26, 1870, Grinnell File.

43. *Ibid.*

44. *Ibid.*

45. Judge William A. Carter, originally from Virginia, was the postmaster and trader at the fort.

46. Dr. James Van A. Carter, the nephew of the Judge, managed the trading store for his uncle.

47. Grinnell, "A Memory of Fort Bridger," Grinnell File, pp. 1–3.

48. Grinnell to Arnold Hague, May 8, 1900, Letter Book, p. 886.

49. Grinnell, "A Memory of Fort Bridger," pp. 3–7.

50. MEMOIRS, p. 42.

51. Grinnell to Richard Sun, May 11, 1921, Letter Book, p. 473.

52. MEMOIRS, p. 42.

53. Grinnell, "An Old-Time Bone Hunt," p. 335.

54. "Ornis" (Grinnell), "The Green River Country," *Forest and Stream* 1 (November 13, 1873):212.

55. *Ibid.*

56. "Uintah" is the older form of Uinta, the spelling preferred today.

57. John Wool Griswold, Yale class of 1871, became an iron manufacturer; James Matson Russell, Yale class of 1870, was an agriculturist from Kentucky; "Joe" or José Alleyo Felemanches, was a Mexican-American who, in addition to cooking and keeping camp, was serving as the party's guide.

58. "Ornis" (Grinnell), "A Day with the Sage Grouse," *Forest and Stream* 1 (November 6, 1873):196.

59. Some of these birds might have been black ducks, but that species

is rarely found this far west; perhaps the birds referred to here were merely hen mallards.

60. "Ornis" (Grinnell), "A Day with the Sage Grouse," p. 196.

61. MEMOIRS, p. 42.

62. *Ibid.*, p. 43.

63. Grinnell to Arnold Hague, May 8, 1900, Letter Book, p. 886.

64. Grinnell, "Sketch of Professor O. C. Marsh," *Popular Science Monthly* (1878) 13:613; Grinnell, "Othniel Charles Marsh, Paleontologist," *Leading American Men of Science,* ed. David Starr Jordan (New York, 1910), p. 293.

65. Schuchert and LeVene, *O. C. Marsh*, p. 247.

66. Goetzmann, *Exploration and Empire*, pp. x–xi.

CHAPTER THREE. HUNTING BUFFALO AND ELK

1. MEMOIRS, p. 44.

2. *Ibid.*

3. *Ibid.*

4. *Ibid.* Over four hundred birds of Grinnell's collection, both skins and mounted specimens, are in the Birdcraft Museum. They include the extinct passenger pigeon and heath hen. "Its [the Museum's] exhibits and study specimens of native birds and mammals have been evaluated by Ralph Morrell of Yale's Peabody Museum. . . as the finest native collection of its kind." *Bridgeport* (Connecticut) *Sunday Post,* April 26, 1964.

5. MEMOIRS, pp. 45–46.

6. "Ornis" (Grinnell), "Buffalo Hunt with the Pawnees," *Forest and Stream* 1 (December 25, 1873):305.

7. *Ibid.*

8. *Ibid.*

9. *Ibid.*

10. In 1871 one Western railroad alone, the Kansas Pacific, shipped to the East the hides, and some meat, of over twenty thousand buffalo; J. A. Allen, *The American Bisons, Living and Extinct. Memoirs of the Museum of Comparative Zoology* 4 (1876):178.

11. The word "lodge" is a synonym for "tepee."

12. Despite his use of the word "ball," Grinnell had a rifle not a smoothbore. He frequently employed "ball" and "bullet" interchangeably.

13. "Ornis" (Grinnell), "Buffalo Hunt with the Pawnees," pp. 305–06.

14. *Ibid.*, p. 306.

15. Grinnell to Robert Bruce, June 20, 1929, Letter Book, p. 473.

16. Grinnell, *Pawnee Hero Stories and Folk Tales* (New York, 1889), p. 301.

17. "Ornis" (Grinnell), "Buffalo Hunt with the Pawnees," p. 306.

18. *Ibid.*

19. Grinnell, *Pawnee Hero Stories and Folk Tales,* p. 302.

20. Grinnell to George E. Hyde, November 4, 1921, Letter Book, p. 883.

21. MEMOIRS, pp. 47–49.

22. For Grinnell's comment on the identity of the Indians, see *Ibid.,* p. 47.

23. By "dugout," Grinnell is probably referring here to a rough shelter formed by digging out the face of a hill or stream bank.

24. MEMOIRS, pp. 49–50.

25. Robert Bruce, *The Fighting Norths and Pawnee Scouts* (Lincoln, Nebraska, 1932), p. 15.

26. Grinnell to Luther North, July 2, 1929, Letter Book, p. 495.

27. MEMOIRS, p. 49.

28. *Ibid.,* p. 50.

29. "Ornis" (Grinnell), "Elk Hunting in Nebraska," *Forest and Stream* 1 (October 2, 1873):116.

30. *Ibid.*

31. *Ibid.*

32. *Ibid.*

33. *Ibid.*

34. *Ibid.*

CHAPTER FOUR. EXPLORING WITH CUSTER

1. In 1872 George B. Grinnell and Company purchased 42,800 shares of Union Pacific Railroad stock; Charles Edgar Ames, *Pioneering the Union Pacific: A Reappraisal of the Builders of the Railroad* (New York, 1969), p. 401. I am indebted to Barry B. Combs of the Union Pacific Railroad Company for pointing out this fact.

2. The depression was the worst the nation had experienced up to that time. Precipitated by the failure of the banking house of Jay Cooke on the eighteenth, the Panic of 1873 was mainly the result of unrestrained speculation in railroad construction. By their manipulation of huge amounts of stock, the Grinnells must assume a part of the responsibility for bringing on the crisis.

3. MEMOIRS, pp. 50–52.

4. *Ibid.,* p. 52.

5. *Ibid.*

6. Luther North had some experience along this line; on Grinnell's recommendation he had collected fossils for Marsh in Colorado in 1873. See Grinnell, *Two Great Scouts and Their Pawnee Battalion* (Cleveland, 1928), p. 236; and Donald F. Danker, ed., *Man of the Plains: Recollections of Luther North, 1856–1882* (Lincoln, Nebraska, 1961), p. 183.

7. MEMOIRS, pp. 52–53.

8. Despite the fact that Custer is often referred to as "General" at the time of the Black Hills exploration, he was actually a colonel. During the Civil War, he had been brevetted major general, but in the postwar reorganization he was given the rank of lieutenant colonel. Nevertheless, he was still known by many — including Grinnell — as "General."

9. MEMOIRS, p. 53.

10. Grinnell, "From Notebooks of Black Hills Expedition — Introduction," Grinnell File, p. 5.

11. North stated: "I believe that Charley Reynolds was the best scout in the West"; Danker, ed., *Man of the Plains*, p. 184.

12. Grinnell, "Charley Reynolds," *Forest and Stream* 47 (December 26, 1896): 503.

13. MEMOIRS, pp. 53–54.

14. Grinnell, "Charley Reynolds," p. 503.

15. MEMOIRS, pp. 54–55.

16. For a discussion of the battle and the number of men killed on both sides, see Jay Monaghan, *The Book of the American West* (New York, 1963 and 1969), pp. 228–29.

17. MEMOIRS, p. 55.

18. Though living in a different part of the West, the Arikaras or Rees were of the same linguistic stock as the Pawnees.

19. MEMOIRS, pp. 56–57.

20. Grinnell, *Two Great Scouts*, p. 240.

21. William Ludlow, *Report of a Reconnaissance of the Black Hills of Dakota, Made in the Summer of 1874* (Washington, D. C., 1875), p. 8.

22. Schuchert and LeVene, *O. C. Marsh*, p. 141; Goetzmann, *Exploration and Empire*, p. 419.

23. MEMOIRS, p. 54.

24. *Ibid.*, pp. 57–58.

25. Ludlow, *Report of a Reconnaissance of the Black Hills*, pp. 8–10.

26. The term "bug hunters" is found in a letter by Edward S. Godfrey, a first lieutenant at the time of the expedition, to Grinnell, September 13, 1894. When I saw it, the letter was in the possession of the late Mrs. John P. Holman, Fairfield, Connecticut.

27. Custer to Assistant Adjutant General, Department of Dakota, July 15, 1874, "Pages from Black Hills Expedition Order and Despatch Book," Beinecke Rare Book and Manuscript Library, Yale University, p. 31.

28. MEMOIRS, p. 59.

29. *Ibid.*, pp. 59–60.

30. By "black-tailed deer," Grinnell is presumably referring to mule deer. White-tailed deer are also found in the Black Hills.

31. MEMOIRS, pp. 58–59.

32. *Ibid.*, p. 57.

33. *Ibid.*, p. 60.

34. *Ibid.*

35. *Ibid.,* pp. 60–61.

36. Literally translated, the bugle call "Stables" signaled the men to "go to the stables," either in the morning or evening, to groom their horses and get them ready either for a day's march or a night's rest. "Reveille," signaling the men to rise, is, of course, the first bugle call of the day.

37. "Boots and Saddles" is the bugle call to mount up.

38. The more common spelling of this segment of the Sioux nation is "Oglala[s]."

39. Red Cloud is one of the most famous Indian leaders, particularly well known for his opposition to government proposals to construct forts along the Bozeman Trail in the 1860's. He engaged U.S. troops so successfully that the government abandoned the trail in 1868. At the time of the Black Hills expedition, he was living peaceably on the Red Cloud Agency in northwestern Nebraska.

40. It may seem strange that Indians "from" a reservation in Nebraska were hunting and camping in the Black Hills, but it should be remembered that in this period so-called "agency Indians" often came and went as they pleased. In one of his despatches from the Hills, Custer complained of this very thing; see Cleophas C. O'Harra, "Custer's Black Hills Expedition of 1874," *Black Hills Engineer* 17 (November, 1929): 261–63.

41. The prisoner was "carried around with us . . . for a few days and then one night crept out under the wall of the tent he was in and . . . disappeared"; Grinnell to J. W. Schultz, June 14, 1923, Letter Book, p. 24A.

42. Grinnell, "From Notebooks of Black Hills Expedition," entry of July 26, 1874, Grinnell File, pp. 1–11.

43. *Ibid.,* pp. 11–12.

44. *Ibid.,* p. 13.

45. *Ibid.,* pp. 13–14. Here is a first-hand account, from dated notebooks, of the discovery of gold in the Black Hills, which places that discovery at least four days earlier than heretofore determined. It seems that Horatio Nelson Ross *did* make the find, as previously thought, but that he kept it secret for several days because he was worried about the effect of the news on the soldiers.

For a discussion of when the "first colors" were found, see Cleophas C. O'Harra, "The Discovery of Gold in the Black Hills," *Black Hills Engineer* 17 (November, 1929): 286–98; W. M. Wemett, "Custer's Expedition to the Black Hills in 1874," *North Dakota Historical Quarterly* 6 (1932): 299; and Donald Jackson, *Custer's Gold: The United States Cavalry Expedition of 1874* (New Haven, 1966 and 1967), pp. 81–85.

46. Grinnell, "From Notebooks of Black Hills Expedition," entry of July 26, 1874, Grinnell File, p. 14.

47. *Ibid.*

48. *Ibid.*

49. *Ibid.*, entry of July 27, 1874, pp. 1–4.

50. Actually, Louis Agard was the guide, though his services did not prove of much value.

51. MEMOIRS, p. 63.

52. *Ibid.*, p. 62.

53. *Ibid.*, p. 61.

54. Danker, ed., *Man of the Plains*, p. 187.

55. *Ibid.*

56. Grinnell, *Two Great Scouts*, p. 241.

57. *Ibid.*, pp. 241–42.

58. MEMOIRS, p. 62.

59. Grinnell, *Two Great Scouts*, p. 242.

60. *Ibid.* Grinnell characterized Custer as a man who gave "the impression always of being intensely in himself, somewhat egotistical in fact"; Grinnell to W. H. Power, November 2, 1927, Letter Book, p. 626.

61. Ludlow, *Report of a Reconnaissance of the Black Hills*, p. 18.

62. This complaint is found in *Ibid.*, p. 75.

63. The plains wolf and Bad Lands bighorn are extinct. The grizzly bears living in the Black Hills region in 1874 may also have been part of a now extinct subspecies.

64. Ludlow, *Report of a Reconnaissance of the Black Hills*, p. 79.

65. *Ibid.*, pp. 79–84.

66. *Ibid.*, p. 83.

67. MEMOIRS, p. 64.

CHAPTER FIVE. INSPECTING THE "NATIONAL PARK"

1. On page 25 of the *Ninth Annual Report of the Sheffield Scientific School of Yale College* (New Haven, 1874), Marsh included the following statement: "Mr. G. B. Grinnell . . . has rendered important aid toward increasing the collection in this [geology] department."

2. MEMOIRS, p. 64.

3. *Ibid.*

4. Hiram Martin Chittenden, *The Yellowstone National Park* (Cincinnati, 1905), pp. 44–51.

5. *Ibid.*, p. 60.

6. Roderick Nash, *Wilderness and the American Mind* (New Haven, 1967), pp. 112–13.

7. John Ise, *Our National Park Policy, A Critical History* (Baltimore, 1961), pp. 21–22.

8. MEMOIRS, pp. 64–65; Grinnell to J. E. Remburg, July 9, 1915, Letter Book, p. 25.

9. William Ludlow, *Report of a Reconnaissance from Carroll, Mon-*

tana Territory, on the Upper Missouri, to the Yellowstone National Park, and Return, Made in the Summer of 1875 (Washington, D. C., 1876), pp. 11–12 and 95. MEMOIRS, p. 65.

10. *Ibid.*

11. Grinnell to C. Hart Merriam, March 27, 1913, Letter Book, p. 882.

12. MEMOIRS, pp. 65–66.

13. Grinnell to E. W. Nelson, May 11, 1916, Letter Book, p. 116.

14. MEMOIRS, p. 66.

15. James Wilson, "Journal of a Trip to the Yellowstone Park, July, August and September, 1875," entry of July 20, Beinecke Rare Book and Manuscript Library, Yale University, p. 25.

16. MEMOIRS, pp. 66–67.

17. *Ibid.*, p. 67.

18. A bison-hunting plains tribe of Algonquian stock, the Piegans were part of the Blackfoot confederacy.

19. MEMOIRS, pp. 67–69.

20. Like the Pawnees, the Crows had long been friendly to the whites, and they often joined U.S. soldiers to fight Sioux and Cheyennes.

21. MEMOIRS, p. 69.

22. *Ibid.*, pp. 69–70.

23. *Ibid.*, pp. 70–71.

24. As glory was war's objective, the Plains Indians quantified honor by the system of "counting coups." These were awarded not just for killing but for feats of daring, such as stealing a horse or touching an armed enemy with a hand, rifle, or coup stick.

25. MEMOIRS, p. 71.

26. *Ibid.*

27. *Ibid.*, pp. 71–72.

28. M. M. Quaife, ed., *'Yellowstone Kelly,' the Memoirs of Luther S. Kelly* (New Haven, 1926), p. 117.

29. MEMOIRS, p. 72.

30. Grinnell to W. H. Power, November 2, 1927, Letter Book, p. 627. For another statement of Grinnell's feeling for Ludlow, see Grinnell to General E. S. Godfrey, October 15, 1914, *Ibid.*, p. 935.

31. Cleophas C. O'Harra, "Custer's Black Hills Expedition of 1874," pp. 261–63; Ludlow, *Report of a Reconnaissance of the Black Hills*, p. 18.

32. Ludlow, *Report of a Reconnaissance from Carroll, Montana Territory, on the Upper Missouri, to the Yellowstone National Park*, p. 37.

33. *Ibid.*, p. 61.

34. MEMOIRS, pp. 72–73.

35. Grinnell, "Charley Reynolds," pp. 503–04.

36. MEMOIRS, pp. 73–74.

37. Grinnell to E. W. Nelson, May 11, 1916, Letter Book, p. 118; Grinnell, "Mountain Sheep," *Journal of Mammalogy* 9 (February, 1928):2.

38. Grinnell to E. W. Nelson, May 11, 1916, Letter Book, pp. 118–19.

39. Grinnell, "The Mountain Sheep and Its Range," *American Big Game in Its Haunts*, ed. Grinnell (New York, 1904), p. 348. He considered this animal "the finest of all our American big game"; *Ibid.*, p. 270.

40. MEMOIRS, p. 74.

41. *Ibid.*

42. *Ibid.*

43. Chittenden, *The Yellowstone National Park*, pp. 86–87.

CHAPTER SIX. COLLECTING ARTIFACTS, FOSSILS, AND TROPHIES

1. MEMOIRS, pp. 74–75.

2. Grinnell, "A Visit to Santa Barbara," Grinnell File.

3. MEMOIRS, p. 75.

4. Grinnell, "A Visit to Santa Barbara," Grinnell File.

5. MEMOIRS, p. 75.

6. The correct spelling is *Cieneguitas*, a Spanish word meaning "little swamps." About four miles west of what is today the center of Santa Barbara, the "area became widely known among archaeologists beginning with David Banks Rogers in 1924, because artifacts and burial places were discovered there which definitely proved the existence of the three Indian cultures of the Santa Barbara Coastal Plain: the Oak Grove, the Hunters, and the Canaliños," Robert B. Gates (Santa Barbara Historical Society) to editor, July 27, 1971. Evidently, Grinnell's earlier work had been forgotten.

7. Grinnell, "A Visit to Santa Barbara," Grinnell File.

8. *Ibid.*

9. MEMOIRS, pp. 75–76.

10. *Ibid.*, p. 76.

11. *Ibid.*

12. *Ibid.*

13. *Ibid.*; Grinnell to P. E. Byrne, April 17, 1923, Letter Book, p. 936.

14. MEMOIRS, p. 77.

15. This account is the result of Grinnell's talks with the Cheyenne victors, the white survivors, and the Indian allies of the whites. Billy Jackson, who had been with Reynolds and Grinnell on the 1874 Black Hills expedition, was a scout for Reno in 1876 and saw Reynolds die. See Grinnell, "Charley Reynolds," p. 504; Grinnell to J. W. Schultz, June 14, 1923, Letter Book, p. 24A; Grinnell to P. E. Byrne, April 17, 1923, *Ibid.*, pp. 936–37; Grinnell to William O. Taylor, February 16, 1916, *Ibid.*, p. 764.

With General Edward S. Godfrey, who had been a first lieutenant on the Black Hills expedition, and two others, Grinnell followed the Custer trail in the summer of 1916 "and reached the battlefield on the same day of the week and the same hour of the day, just forty years after Custer rode over the hill to his defeat." Grinnell then had the melancholy task of placing a marker on the spot where Reynolds fell; Grinnell to Capt. John Ryan, May 3, 1922, *Ibid.*, p. 376; Grinnell to Edward Sawyer, January 23, 1917, *Ibid.*, p. 7.

16. MEMOIRS, p. 77.

17. Charles Hallock, "In the Beginning," *Forest and Stream* 40 (June 29, 1893):559.

18. Grinnell to Charles Sheldon, March 4, 1925, Grinnell File.

19. Charles Hallock to Grinnell, October 11, 1876, Grinnell File.

20. *Ibid.*

21. MEMOIRS, p. 77.

22. Charles Hallock to Grinnell, October 11, 1876, Grinnell File.

23. MEMOIRS, p. 78. *The Sportsman's Gazetteer and General Guide; The Game Animals, Birds and Fishes of North America: Their Habits and Various Methods of Capture; Copious Instructions in Shooting, Fishing, Taxidermy, Woodcraft, Etc., Together with a Directory to the Principal Game Resorts of the Country, Illustrated with Maps* appeared in 1877 under Charles Hallock's name and was a standard source for years. In reality, four others did the work while Hallock took the credit. Grinnell wrote the section on mammals and birds, 229 pages out of the total of 896. See MEMOIRS, pp.77-78; in addition, "Genesis of Hallock's Sportsman's Gazetteer as Recalled by George Bird Grinnell, October 31, 1922," which I examined when in the possession of the late Mrs. John P. Holman, Fairfield, Connecticut, also documents this point.

24. Grinnell to Editor, *Greenfield* [Mass.] *Gazette and Courier*, May 22, 1903, Letter Book, pp. 75–76.

25. MEMOIRS, pp. 78–80.

26. *Ibid.*, pp. 80–81.

27. This is the famous monograph on the extinct toothed birds praised by Darwin; see Chapter Two, above. For this and other aid given by Grinnell, Marsh named a fossil after him: *Crocodilus grinnelli*; Schuchert and LeVene, *O. C. Marsh*, p. 298.

28. Actually, Carlin and Reed together wrote, rather than visited, Marsh to tell him of their discovery; *Ibid.*, pp. 196–97.

Near the town is the extensive Como Bluffs region; "it was along the foot of these bluffs that the various quarries [later] operated by Marsh were located"; *Ibid.*, pp. 202–03.

29. MEMOIRS, pp. 83–84.

30. Grinnell, *Two Great Scouts*, pp. 286–87.

31. *Ibid.*, p. 287.

32. MEMOIRS, pp. 81–82.

33. *Ibid.*, p. 82.

34. *Ibid.*, p. 83.

35. Charles Hallock to Grinnell, September 28, 1878, Grinnell File.

36. MEMOIRS, p. 83.

37. The editor has been unable to discover the names of these two men, but they were probably relatives of Grinnell.

38. "Yo" (Grinnell), "A Trip to North Park" (Fourth Paper), *Forest and Stream* 13 (September 25, 1879): 670.

39. *Ibid.*, p. 671.

40. *Ibid.*

41. Among the many countries that utilize fire regularly to improve their land is South Africa. There, the rangers of the great national parks employ this tool to increase the grassland's productivity for herbivores.

42. "Yo" (Grinnell), "A Trip to North Park" (Fifth Paper), *Forest and Stream* 13 (October 2, 1879): 691.

43. *Ibid.*

44. *Ibid.*

45. MEMOIRS, pp. 85–86.

46. "Yo" (Grinnell), "A Trip to North Park" (Fifth Paper), p. 691; Grinnell to E. W. Nelson, May 11, 1916, Letter Book, p. 117.

47. Grinnell, "Pronghorn Antelope," *Journal of Mammalogy* 10 (May, 1929):138.

48. "Yo" (Grinnell), "A Trip to North Park" (Fifth Paper), p. 691.

49. "Yo" (Grinnell), "A Trip to North Park" (Sixth Paper), *Forest and Stream* 13 (October 9, 1879): 711.

50. "Yo" (Grinnell), "A Trip to North Park" (Seventh Paper), *Ibid.* 13 (October 16, 1879): 730.

51. *Ibid.*, p. 731.

52. The more common spelling of these rude Indian huts, made usually of brushwood, is "wickiup."

53. "Yo" (Grinnell), "A Trip to North Park" (Eighth Paper), *Forest and Stream* 13 (October 23, 1879): 752.

54. MEMOIRS, p. 86.

55. "Yo" (Grinnell), "A Trip to North Park" (Eighth Paper), p. 752.

56. Robert E. Riegel and Robert G. Athearn, *America Moves West* (New York, 1971), p. 466.

57. "Yo" (Grinnell), "A Trip to North Park" (Eighth Paper), p. 751.

58. "Yo" (Grinnell), "A Trip to North Park" (Concluding Paper), *Forest and Stream* 14 (October 30, 1879):771.

59. *Ibid.*

60. *Ibid.*

61. MEMOIRS, pp. 86–87.

62. *Ibid.*, p. 87; Grinnell To Charles Sheldon, March 4, 1925, Grinnell File.

63. MEMOIRS, p. 87.

64. *Ibid.*

65. *Ibid.*

66. *Ibid.*, p. 88.

67. *Ibid.*

68. *Ibid.*, p. 89.

69. "Yo" (Grinnell), "Bye-Ways of the Northwest" (First Paper), *Forest and Stream* 16 (July 14, 1881): 469.

70. Fannin was later curator of the Provincial Museum in Victoria.

71. MEMOIRS, pp. 89–90.

72. *Ibid.*, p. 90.

73. "Yo" (Grinnell), "Bye-Ways of the Northwest" (Twelfth Paper), *Forest and Stream* 18 (February 9, 1882): 25.

74. *Ibid.*

75. *Ibid.*

76. *Ibid.*

77. *Ibid.*

78. *Ibid.*

79. *Ibid.*

80. *Ibid.*

81. MEMOIRS, pp. 90–91.

82. *Ibid.*, p. 90.

83. "Yo" (Grinnell), "Bye-Ways of the Northwest" (Twelfth Paper), p. 25.

84. *Ibid.*

85. *Ibid.*

86. MEMOIRS, p. 91.

87. "Yo" (Grinnell), "Bye-Ways of the Northwest" (Twelfth Paper), p. 25.

88. MEMOIRS, p. 91.

89. *Ibid.*, pp. 91–92.

90. "Yo" (Grinnell), "Bye-Ways of the Northwest" (Twelfth Paper), p. 25.

91. MEMOIRS, p. 92.

92. "Yo" (Grinnell), "A Trip to North Park" (Concluding Paper), p. 771.

EPILOGUE

1. Grinnell, *Two Great Scouts,* p. 288.

2. MEMOIRS, pp. 96–97.

3. *Ibid.,* p. 97. Finally, about 1903, Grinnell parted with what had proved to be a disastrous investment; Grinnell to Charles Hallock, March 21, 1903, Letter Book, p. 931.

4. See Madison Grant's pamphlet on the *Early History of Glacier National Park Montana* (Washington, D.C., 1919).

5. Grinnell to John Willis, January 11, 1916, Letter Book, p. 634.

6. *Ibid.*

7. "Yo" (Grinnell), "A Load of Meat," *Forest and Stream* 21 (October 18, 1883):223.

8. *Ibid.*

9. The only "uncontrolled" Indians after 1883 were the Arizona Apaches under Geronimo, who escaped his white captors in that year and remained at large until 1886.

For the fact that the last of the large buffalo herds passed away in the fall of 1883, see Wayne Gard, *The Great Buffalo Hunt* (New York, 1959), 274.

Selected Bibliography

PRIMARY SOURCES

Manuscripts

Custer, General George Armstrong. "Pages from the Black Hills Expedition Order and Despatch Book," July 1 to August 25, 1874. Yale University Beinecke Rare Book and Manuscript Library.
Grinnell, George Bird. Collection of Journals, Field Notes and other Materials on the Plains Indians, 1870–1930. Southwest Museum Library, Los Angeles, California.
——. Grinnell File. Formerly at Birdcraft Museum of the Connecticut Audubon Society, now at Yale University.
——. Letter Books, August 2, 1886 to October 17, 1929. Formerly at Birdcraft Museum, now at Yale University.
——. Letters and other papers in the possession of the late Mrs. John P. Holman, Fairfield, Connecticut.
Roosevelt, Theodore. Papers. Washington, D.C.: U.S. Library of Congress, Manuscript Division.
Wilson, James. "Journal of a Trip to the Yellowstone Park, July, August and September, 1875." Yale University Beinecke Rare Book and Manuscript Library.

Miscellaneous Contemporary Writings

Allen, Joel A. *The American Bisons, Living and Extinct. Memoirs of the Museum of Comparative Zoology.* Vol. 4 (1876). Cambridge: Harvard University Press.

Brown, Dee, ed. *Pawnee, Blackfeet and Cheyenne: History and Folklore of the Plains from the Writings of George Bird Grinnell.* New York: Charles Scribner's Sons, 1961.

Danker, Donald F., ed. *Man of the Plains: Recollections of Luther North, 1856–1882.* Lincoln: University of Nebraska Press, 1961.

Forest and Stream. 77 volumes. August 14, 1873 to December 30, 1911.

Grinnell, George Bird, ed. *American Big Game in Its Haunts.* New York: Forest and Stream Publishing Company, 1904.

————. *American Duck Shooting.* New York: Forest and Stream Publishing Company, 1901.

————. *American Game-Bird Shooting.* New York: Forest and Stream Publishing Company, 1910.

————, ed. *Audubon Magazine* 1 (February, 1887 to January, 1888).

————. *Audubon Park: The History of the Site of the Hispanic Society of America and Neighboring Institutions.* New York: Hispanic Society of America, 1927.

————. *Blackfoot Indian Stories.* New York: Charles Scribner's Sons, 1914.

————. *Blackfoot Lodge Tales: The Story of a Prairie People.* Lincoln: University of Nebraska Press, 1962. (First published in 1892: New York, Charles Scribner's Sons.)

————. *By Cheyenne Campfires.* New Haven: Yale University Press, 1962. (First published by Yale in 1926.)

————, ed. "A Chapter of History and Natural History in Old New York." *Natural History* 20 (1920): 23–27.

————. *The Cheyenne Indians — Their History and Ways of Life.* 2 vols. New York: Cooper Square Publishers, 1962. (First published in 1923: New Haven, Yale University Press.)

————. *The Fighting Cheyennes.* Norman: University of Oklahoma Press, 1956. (First published in 1915: New York, Charles Scribner's Sons.)

————, ed. *Hunting at High Altitudes.* New York: Harper & Brothers, 1913.

————. *The Indians of Today.* New York: Duffield, 1911. (First published in 1900: New York, Herbert S. Stone.)

————. "Mountain Sheep." *Journal of Mammalogy* 9 (February, 1928): 1–9.

————. "Notice of a New Genus of Annelids from the Lower Silurian." *American Journal of Science and Arts* 14 (September, 1877): 1–2.

————. "An Old-Time Bone Hunt." *Natural History* 23 (1923): 329–36.

————. "Old-Time Range of Virginia Deer, Moose and Elk." *Natural History* 25 (1925): 136–42.

————. "On a New Crinoid from the Cretaceous Formation of the West." *American Journal of Science and Arts,* 12 (July, 1876): 81–83.

————. "Othniel Charles Marsh, Paleontologist." *Leading American Men of Science,* ed. David Starr Jordan, pp. 283–312. New York: Henry Holt, 1910.

————. *Pawnee Hero Stories and Folk Tales; With Notes on the Origins, Customs and Character of the Pawnee People.* Lincoln: University of Nebraska Press, 1961. (First published in 1889: New York, Forest and Stream Publishing Company.)

————. "Pronghorn Antelope." *Journal of Mammalogy* 10 (May, 1929): 135–41.

————. *The Punishment of the Stingy and Other Indian Stories.* New York: Harper and Brothers, 1901.

————. "Recollections of Audubon Park." *Auk* 37 (July, 1920): 372–80.

————. "Review of Professor Marsh's Monograph on the *Odontornithes,* or Toothed Birds of North America." *American Journal of Science* 21 (April, 1881): 255–76.

————. "Sketch of Professor O. C. Marsh." *Popular Science Monthly* 13 (1878): 612–17.

————. *The Story of the Indian.* New York: D. Appleton, 1895 and 1898.

————. *Two Great Scouts and Their Pawnee Battalion.* Cleveland: Arthur H. Clark, 1928.

————. *When Buffalo Ran.* Norman: University of Oklahoma Press, 1966. (First published in 1920: New Haven, Yale University Press.)

————, and Dana, Edward S. "On a New Tertiary Lake Basin." *American Journal of Science and Arts* 11 (February, 1876): 126–28.

Hallock, Charles. *The Sportsman's Gazetteer and General Guide; The Game Animals, Birds and Fishes of North America: Their Habits and Various Methods of Capture; Copious Instructions in Shooting, Fishing, Taxidermy, Woodcraft, Etc., Together with a Directory to the Principal Game Resorts of the Country, Illustrated with Maps.* New York: Forest and Stream Publishing Company, 1877.

Johnson, Willis Fletcher, ed. *Addresses and Papers of Theodore Roosevelt.* New York: Unit Book Publishing Company, 1909.

Ludlow, William. *Report of a Reconnaissance from Carroll, Montana Territory, on the Upper Missouri, to the Yellowstone National Park, and Return, Made in the Summer of 1875.* Washington, D.C.: Government Printing Office, 1876.

————. *Report of a Reconnaissance of the Black Hills of Dakota, Made in the Summer of 1874.* Washington, D.C.: Government Printing Office, 1875.

Merriam, C. Hart. *A Review of the Birds of Connecticut.* New Haven: Tuttle, Morehouse and Taylor, 1877.

Morison, Elting E., and Blum, John M., eds. *The Letters of Theodore Roosevelt.* 8 vols. Cambridge: Harvard University Press, 1951–54.

Ninth Annual Report of the Sheffield Scientific School of Yale College. New Haven: Sheffield Scientific School, 1874.

Quaife, M. M., ed. *'Yellowstone Kelly.' The Memoirs of Luther S. Kelly.* New Haven: Yale University Press, 1926.

Roosevelt, Theodore. *Works.* Memorial Edition. 24 vols. New York: Charles Scribner's Sons, 1923–26.

——. *Works.* National Edition. 20 vols. New York: Charles Scribner's Sons, 1926.

——, and Grinnell, George Bird, eds. *American Big-Game Hunting.* New York: Forest and Stream Publishing Company, 1893.

——, and ——. *Hunting in Many Lands.* New York: Forest and Stream Publishing Company, 1895.

——, and ——. *Trail and Camp-Fire.* New York: Forest and Stream Publishing Company, 1897.

Whitney, Caspar, Grinnell, George Bird, and Wister, Owen, eds. *Musk-Ox, Bison, Sheep and Goat.* New York: Macmillan, 1904.

Wildwood, Will, ed. *Frank Forester's Sporting Scenes and Characters.* 2 vols. Philadelphia: T. B. Peterson and Brothers, 1881.

SECONDARY SOURCES

General Histories

Matthiessen, Peter. *Wildlife in America.* New York: Viking Press, 1959, 1964 and 1967.

Mead, Margaret, and Bunzel, Ruth L. *The Golden Age of American Anthropology.* New York: George Braziller, 1960.

Monaghan, Jay, ed. *The Book of the American West.* New York: Simon and Schuster, 1963 and 1969.

Riegel, Robert E., and Athearn, Robert G. *America Moves West.* New York: Holt, Rinehart & Winston, 1930, 1947, 1956, 1964, and 1971.

Monographs and Special Studies

Ames, Charles Edgar. *Pioneering the Union Pacific; A Reappraisal of the Builders of the Railroad.* New York: Appleton-Century-Crofts, 1969.

Bruce, Robert. *The Fighting Norths and Pawnee Scouts.* Lincoln, Nebraska: Nebraska State Historical Society, 1932.

Chittenden, Hiram Martin. *The Yellowstone National Park.* Cincinnati: Robert Clark, 1905.

Cochran, Thomas C. *Railroad Leaders, 1845–1890: The Business Mind in Action.* Cambridge: Harvard University Press, 1953.

Goetzmann, William H. *Exploration and Empire: The Explorer and the Scientist in the Winning of the West.* New York: Alfred A. Knopf, 1966.

Grant, Madison. *Early History of Glacier National Park Montana.* Washington, D.C.: Government Printing Office, 1919.

Grinnell, George Bird, and Sheldon, Charles, eds. *Hunting and Conservation.* New Haven: Yale University Press, 1925.

——, Roosevelt, Kermit, Cross, W. Redmond, and Gray, Prentiss N., eds. *Hunting Trails on Three Continents.* New York: Windward House, 1933.

Herrick, Francis Hobart. *Audubon the Naturalist; A History of His Life and Times.* 2 vols. New York: D. Appleton, 1917.

Ise, John. *Our National Park Policy: A Critical History.* Baltimore: Johns Hopkins University Press, 1961.

Jackson, Donald. *Custer's Gold: The United States Cavalry Expedition of 1874.* New Haven: Yale University Press, 1966 and 1967.

Nash, Roderick. *Wilderness and the American Mind.* New Haven: Yale University Press, 1967 and 1973.

O'Harra, Cleophas C. "Custer's Black Hills Expedition of 1874." *Black Hills Engineer* 17 (November, 1929): 221–86.

——. "The Discovery of Gold in the Black Hills." *Black Hills Engineer* 17 (November, 1929): 286–98.

Reiger, John F. *American Sportsmen and the Origins of Conservation.* New York: Winchester Press, 1975.

——. "A Dedication to the Memory of George Bird Grinnell, 1849-1938." *Arizona and the West* 21 (Spring, 1979): 1-4.

——. "George Bird Grinnell." *National Wildlife* 11 (February-March, 1973): 12-13.

——. "Grinnell, George Bird (1849-1938)." *Encyclopedia of American Forest and Conservation History.* New York: Macmillan, 1983.

Robinson, Donald H. *Through the Years in Glacier National Park.* West Glacier, Montana: Glacier Natural History Association, 1960.

Saveth, Edward N. "The American Patrician Class: A Field for Research." *American Quarterly* 15 (Summer, 1963): 235-52.

Schuchert, Charles and LeVene, Clara Mae. *O. C. Marsh, Pioneer in Paleontology.* New Haven: Yale University Press, 1940.

Trefethen, James B. *Crusade for Wildlife: Highlights in Conservation Progress.* Harrisburg, Pennsylvania: Stackpole Books, 1961.

Index

Ludlow, William, 1, 80, 85, 103, 105, 107, 108, 109, 110, 111, 117, 118, 119, 165 *n*
Macomb's Dam (New York), 21
Macomb's Dam Bridge, 20
Madison Square Garden, 8
Manhattanville, New York, 9
Marsh, O. C., 1, 29, 30, 31, 33, 34, 35, 36, 38, 43, 46, 51, 54, 55, 56, 58, 80, 107, 108, 109, 122, 123, 125, 130, 143, 158 *n*, 161 *n*, 164 *n*, 167 *n*
Mass, Phil, 44, 45
Massachusetts, 9, 127
Massengale, 151
Mather, Fred, 143
Maxwell, Nebraska, 33
McIntosh, Donald, 84
McKay, William T., 84, 94, 101
meadowlark, 17, 60
Medicine Bow, Wyoming, 130
Melrose, Montana, 148
Merriam, C. Hart, 108
Middle Park, Colorado, 133, 139, 140
Milford, Connecticut, 108, 121, 124, 125, 126, 132
Minnesota, 80, 85, 107, 109, 158 *n;* University of, 105
Mirror Lake (British Columbia), 145
Missoula, Montana, 148
Montana, 1, 2-3, 84, 98, 100, 108, 109, 110, 111, 112, 113, 114-16, 117, 118, 119, 120, 121, 125, 126, 147, 148, 151, 166 *n*
Morrell, Ralph, 160 *n*
Morris House (Hotel), 123
Moscow, Russia, 26
Mount Tom (Massachusetts), 9
Mountains, Bighorn, 96
  Coeur D'Alene, 146
  Little Rocky, 119
  Moccasin, 119
  Rocky, 130, 138, 142
  Sierra Nevada, 123, 124
  Snowy, 135, 136, 137
  Uinta, 50
Moylan, Myles, 84
Museum, Birdcraft, 4, 154 *n*, 156 *n*, 160 *n;* Provincial, 169 *n;* Peabody, 55, 58, 80, 108, 122, 124, 125, 126, 127, 143, 160 *n*
muskrat, 20
Nanaimo, British Columbia, 145
National Parks, Glacier, 151, 170 *n;*

Rocky Mountain, 133; Yellowstone, 109, 110, 117, 118, 119, 121, 148
Naugatuck Junction, Connecticut, 132
Nebraska, 29, 31, 32, 33, 34, 35-38, 58, 59-60, 61, 62, 63, 64, 69, 70, 71, 72, 73, 74, 75, 76, 77, 79, 127, 128, 129, 130, 131, 132, 133, 142, 144, 150, 152, 163 *n*
New Haven, Connecticut, 27, 28, 30, 58, 80, 107, 109, 111, 126-27, 133, 143
New Jersey, 8, 9, 12, 20
New Westminster, British Columbia, 145
New York, 6, 8, 9, 10, 12, 14, 15, 16, 17, 18, 19, 20, 21, 26, 30, 87, 110, 132, 156 *n*
New York City, 2, 4, 6, 7, 8, 9, 10-14, 15, 16-19, 20-25, 26, 27, 55, 57, 58, 73, 77, 78, 79, 80, 107, 127, 132, 142, 143, 148, 156 *n*
New York Herald, 83
New York Juvenile Asylum, 14
New York Tribune, 83
New York Zoological Society, 132
Nicholson, John Reed, 30, 38, 39, 40, 41, 48, 49, 50, 51, 52, 53, 159 *n*
North, Frank, 33, 34, 35, 37, 58, 96, 127, 130, 131, 132, 150
North, Luther, 58, 59, 60, 62, 64, 66, 68, 69, 70, 71, 72, 73, 74, 75, 76, 77, 80, 81, 84, 85, 86, 89, 90, 91, 94, 95, 96, 98, 99, 100, 101, 102, 103, 104, 105, 106, 112, 125, 127, 128, 129, 130, 131, 132, 150, 161 *n*
North Park, Colorado, 133, 134, 135, 140, 141, 144
North Platte, Nebraska, 127, 130, 132
Omaha, Nebraska, 32, 73, 152
Oregon, 145, 146
Oregon Trail, 41
osprey, 18, 156 *n*
Ossining, New York, 26
Palisades (New York-New Jersey), 8, 20
Panic of 1873, 79, 161 *n*
Parkin, W., 81
Pass, Muddy, 140; Rabbit Ears, 140
Payne, L. R., 28
Pend Oreille Lake (Idaho), 146, 147
Peta-la-shar, 62
Philadelphia, Pennsylvania, 85